D
CE

JANE AUSTEN

Notes by Martin and Laura Gray
Revised by Emma Page

Longman
is an imprint of

PEARS

YORK PRESS

YORK PRESS
322 Old Brompton Road, London SW5 9JH

PEARSON EDUCATION LIMITED
Edinburgh Gate, Harlow,
Essex CM20 2JE, United Kingdom

Associated companies, branches and representatives throughout the world

First published 1998

New edition 2004

This new and fully revised edition 2013

10 9 8 7 6 5 4 3 2 1

ISBN 978–1–4479–4886–5

Illustration on page 9 by Neil Gower

Phototypeset by Carnegie Book Production

Printed in Italy

Photo credits: © Classic Image/Alamy for page 6 / Nella/Shutterstock.com for page 7 / © Derek Payne/Alamy for page 8 / © Jeff Morgan 06/Alamy for page 10 / Tymonko Galyna/Shutterstock.com for page 11 / Scruggelgreen/Shutterstock.com for page 12 / titov dmitriy/Shutterstock.com for page 13 / Elena Kharichkina/Shutterstock.com for page 14 / Anastasija Popova/Shutterstock.com for page 15 / rebirth3d/Shutterstock.com for page 16 / Jamen Percy/Shutterstock.com for page 18 / Pressmaster/Shutterstock.com for page 19 / Marko Bradic/Shutterstock.com for page 23 top / Sergey Novikov/Shutterstock.com for page 23 bottom / Dream79/Shutterstock.com for page 24 top / Scott Rothstein/Shutterstock.com for page 24 bottom / © Genevieve Vallee/Alamy for page 25 / Yuri Arcurs/Shutterstock.com for page 29 / videodoctor/Shutterstock.com for page 30 / Ambient Ideas/Shutterstock.com for page 34 / Fenton one/Shutterstock.com for page 35 / JeniFoto/Shutterstock.com for page 36 / David Hughes/Shutterstock.com for page 38 / Miramiska/Shutterstock.com for page 39 / ©iStockphoto.com/dem10 for page 41 top / ©iStockphoto.com/Rivendellstudios for page 41 bottom / Standa Riha/Shutterstock.com for page 42 top / Sergios/Shutterstock.com for page 42 middle / ©iStockphoto.com/bluestocking for page 43 / / jannoon02B/Shutterstock.com for page 45 / Gregory Constanzo/Getty Images for page 49 / © LOOK Die Bildagentur der Fotografen GmbH/Alamy for page 50 / © Mark Titterton/Alamy for page 51 / picturepartners/Shutterstock.com for page 53 / © Jeff Morgan 03/Alamy for page 54 middle / conrado/Shutterstock.com for page 54 bottom / albund/Shutterstock.com for page 55 / © Rolf Richardson/Alamy for page 60 / BestPhotoStudio/Shutterstock.com for page 61 / -Markus-/Shutterstock.com for page 62 / LilKar/Shutterstock.com for page 63 / Gabriela Insuratelu/Shutterstock.com for page 64 / StudioSmart/Shutterstock.com for page 65 top / Kerry Garvey/Shutterstock.com for page 65 bottom / Joshua Haviv/Shutterstock.com for page 66 / Olaru Radian-Alexandru/Shutterstock.com for page 67 top / ChinellatoPhoto/Shutterstock.com for page 67 bottom / Sergios/Shutterstock.com for page 68 top / silver-john/Shutterstock.com for page 68 bottom / Dasha Petrenko/Shutterstock.com for page 69 / BestPhotoStudio/Shutterstock.com for page 70 top / Petrenko Andriy/Shutterstock.com for page 70 middle / Dayna More/Shutterstock.com for page 71 / Alexander Saprykin/Shutterstock.com for page 72 top / Malyugin/Shutterstock.com for page 72 bottom / ©iStockphoto.com/jsteck for page 73 / Gregory Constanzo/Getty Images for page 74 / Warrem Goldswain/Shutterstock.com for page 75 top / Pavel Vakhrushev/Shutterstock.com for page 75 bottom / bart78/Shutterstock.com for page 76 top / Tischenko Irina/Shutterstock.com for page 76 bottom / Yuri Arcurs/Shutterstock.com for page 77 / © Jeff Morgan 15/Alamy for page 78 / Africa Studio/Shutterstock.com for page 79 top / Alexander Mak/Shutterstock.com for page 79 bottom / Nick Dolding/Getty Images for page 80 top / © BL Images Ltd/Alamy for page 80 middle / Maryna Pleshkun/Shutterstock.com for page 81 / Africa Studio/Shutterstock.com for page 82 / Anneka/Shutterstock.com for page 83 top / Jane McIlroy/Shutterstock.com for page 83 bottom / artjazz/Shutterstock.com for page 84 top / SvetlanaFedoseyeva/Shutterstock.com for page 84 bottom / © The National Trust Photolibrary/Alamy for page 85 / marekuliasz/Shutterstock.com for page 86 / Dim Dimich/Shutterstock.com for page 87 / taro911 Photographer/Shutterstock.com for page 88 / Palo_ok/Shutterstock.com for page 89 / Yuliya Yafimik/Shutterstock.com for page 91 top / Duncan Payne/Shutterstock.com for page 91 bottom / VMM/Shutterstock.com for page 92 top / iravgustin/Shutterstock.com for page 92 bottom / LanKS/Shutterstock.com for page 93 / mycteria/Shutterstock.com for page 94 / ktdesign/Shutterstock.com for page 95 top / Anetlanda/Shutterstock.com for page 95 bottom / © Falkenstein/Bildagentur-online Historical Collect./Alamy for page 96 top / ©iStockphoto.com/Christina Hanck for page 96 bottom / Denis Vrublevski/Shutterstock.com for page 97 / koya979/Shutterstock.com for page 98 / pjhpix/Shutterstock.com for page 99 top / © The National Trust Photolibrary/Alamy for page 99 middle / Africa Studio/Shutterstock.com for page 99 bottom / Allen Stoner/Shutterstock.com for page 101 top/ © Ruby/Alamy for page 101 middle / Subbotina Anna/Shutterstock.com for page 102 / © The Art Archive/Alamy for page 103 / ©iStockphoto.com/Goldfaery for page 117

CONTENTS

PART ONE: INTRODUCING *PRIDE AND PREJUDICE*

PART TWO: STUDYING *PRIDE AND PREJUDICE*

PART THREE: CHARACTERS AND THEMES

PART FOUR: STRUCTURE, FORM AND LANGUAGE

PART FIVE: CONTEXTS AND CRITICAL DEBATES

PART SIX: GRADE BOOSTER

ESSENTIAL STUDY TOOLS

HOW TO STUDY *PRIDE AND PREJUDICE*

These Notes can be used in a range of ways to help you read, study and (where relevant) revise for your exam or assessment.

READING THE NOVEL

Read the novel once, fairly quickly, for pleasure. This will give you a good sense of the over-arching shape of the narrative, and a good feel for the highs and lows of the action, the pace and tone, and the sequence in which information is withheld or revealed. You could ask yourself:

- How do individual characters change or develop? How do my own responses to them change?
- From whose point of view is the novel told? Does this change or remain the same?
- Are the events presented chronologically, or is the time scheme altered in some way?
- What impression do the locations and settings, such as Meryton and Pemberley, make on my reading and response to the text?
- What sort of language, style and form am I aware of as the novel progresses? Does Austen structure the novel precisely, or is there a more relaxed approach – or both? Does she use imagery, or recurring motifs and symbols?

On your second reading, make detailed notes around the key areas highlighted above and in the Assessment Objectives, such as form, language, structure (AO2), links and connections to other texts (AO3) and the context/background for the novel (AO4). These may seem quite demanding, but these Notes will suggest particular elements to explore or jot down.

INTERPRETING OR CRITIQUING THE NOVEL

Although it's not helpful to think in terms of the novel being 'good' or 'bad', you should consider the different ways the novel can be read. How have critics responded to it? Do their views match yours – or do you take a different viewpoint? Are there different ways you can interpret specific events, characters or settings? This is a key aspect in AO3, and it can be helpful to keep a log of your responses and the various perspectives which are expressed both by established critics, and also by classmates, your teacher, or other readers.

REFERENCES AND SOURCES

You will be expected to draw on critics' comments, or refer to source information from the period or the present. Make sure you make accurate, clear notes of writers or sources you have used, for example noting down titles of works, authors' names, website addresses, dates, etc. You may not have to reference all these things when you respond to a text, but knowing the source of your information will allow you to go back to it, if need be – and to check its accuracy and relevance.

REVISING FOR AND RESPONDING TO AN ASSESSED TASK OR EXAM QUESTION

The structure and the contents of these Notes are designed to help to give you the relevant information or ideas you need to answer tasks you have been set. First, work out the key words or ideas from the task (for example, 'form', 'Volume One, Chapter IX', 'Elizabeth', etc.), then read the relevant parts of the Notes that relate to these terms or words, selecting what is useful for revision or written response. Then, turn to **Part Six: Grade Booster** for help in formulating your actual response.

GRADE BOOSTER A02

Finding good quotations to support your interpretation of the characters will greatly enhance and strengthen your points.

CHECK THE BOOK A01

The York Handbook *Dictionary of Literary Terms*, by Martin Gray, provides explanations of the special vocabulary that will help you understand and write about novels like *Pride and Prejudice*.

PRIDE AND PREJUDICE IN CONTEXT

JANE AUSTEN: LIFE AND TIMES

16 December 1775	Jane Austen born in Steventon, Hampshire, the seventh of eight children
1783–1786	Jane and her sister Cassandra receive their only formal education at schools in Oxford and then Reading
1789	Outbreak of the French Revolution
1790	Jane finishes *Love and Freindship* [sic], a mockery of the distorted passions and conventions of sentimental fiction. She writes a considerable amount of juvenile fiction, mostly **parodies**
1793	France declares war on Britain. Execution of Louis XVI and Marie Antoinette
1796–1797	Jane writes *First Impressions*, the lost original of *Pride and Prejudice*
1801	The family moves to Bath
1802	Jane turns down Harris Bigg-Wither's proposal of marriage
1809	Following the death of her father four years earlier, Jane settles at Chawton in Hampshire with her mother and sister
1811	*Sense and Sensibility* is published, followed by *Pride and Prejudice* in **1813**, *Mansfield Park* in **1814**, and *Emma* in **1815**. They are all published anonymously.
1815	Napoleon is defeated by Wellington at the Battle of Waterloo
1817	Jane dies in Winchester. Her last remaining novels, *Persuasion* and *Northanger Abbey*, are published after her death.

CHECK THE BOOK **A04**

Two useful biographies are David Nokes: *Jane Austen* (1997) and Claire Tomalin: *Jane Austen: A Life* (1997).

GRADE BOOSTER **A04**

As you read, note how much we are told about the characters' exact financial circumstances.

MARRIAGE, MONEY AND MANNERS

Pride and Prejudice is one of the most famous novels in the **canon** of English literature, constantly in print, read and reread since its publication in 1813, and made into numerous films and television adaptations. Essentially it is a love story, though we may be surprised by the frequency with which money is discussed rather than sentiment or powerful feeling.

Elizabeth Bennet has come to be seen as one of the great heroines from the whole range of nineteenth-century novels; intelligent, sympathetic and witty, with an attitude to family life and marriage which is a model of balance, humour and good sense. With her help and some good luck, Mr Darcy, whom she begins by disliking but comes to see in a different light, is rescued from being a snob, with an outlook narrowed by pride in his wealth and ancestry, and turned into a true gentleman.

The novel can be richly enjoyed for its comic world populated by Elizabeth's petty-minded and excitable mother, her father, surrounded by women whom he regards as essentially silly, the boring, pompous Mr Collins, and Lady Catherine de Bourgh, the essence of all haughty self-centredness. The reader can also enjoy piecing together an impression of Austen's art as a **narrator**. The relationships between the characters, and their different reactions to the various **themes** that are introduced throughout the **plot**, are as finely patterned and balanced as her individual sentences and paragraphs. As readers we are led through the maze of manners and behaviour; we are tested and to a certain extent tricked by the appearance of things. This is a novel where from the first sentence **irony** is at play, and we must read carefully so as not to miss the sharp implications of some of Austen's comments.

A NARROW FOCUS?

The focus of *Pride and Prejudice* is very narrowly domestic. The famous opening sentence makes a mock 'universal truth' out of the greedy husband-searching in a village where there only seem to be daughters. Love and marriage are the main sources of interest for the inhabitants of Meryton and its environs. They seem untouched by history, politics or social and industrial change. Can the novel really have been published only sixteen years after the French Revolution, at a time when Britain was at war with France and the Napoleonic wars were raging over Europe? The arrival of the militia in Meryton hints at political events, but this is not explained or dwelt on. From within the narrow framework, we see nothing of the agricultural year, the running of the households, the poverty or otherwise of ordinary villagers. There is no vivid sense of a wider world than Meryton, Hunsford and Pemberley, with just the occasional mention of the districts of London and of London society.

The narrowness of Jane Austen's interests as a novelist has been a source of both criticism and praise. She described her material herself in letters: '3 or 4 families in a Country Village is the very thing to work on' (to Anna Austen, September 1814). In another description she uses an image of miniaturist painting ('a little bit (two Inches wide) of Ivory on which I work with so fine a brush', to J. Edward Austen, 16 December 1816). But some have seen the restrictions of Austen's subject matter as a source of strength and exactitude. One of Austen's early admirers was Sir Walter Scott, a novelist who took on the largest themes of history and politics: rereading *Pride and Prejudice*, he remarks in his *Journal* on Austen's 'talent for describing the involvements, and feelings, and characters of ordinary life, which is to me the most wonderful I ever met with'.

> **CONTEXT** **A04**
>
> Miniature pictures on ivory are on display in Jane Austen's house in Chawton, Hampshire, now a museum.

STUDY FOCUS: READING THEN AND NOW **A03**

We may find it difficult to sympathise with a society in which the sole function of middle-class women seems to be to marry as 'well' as possible and where the rich and powerful expect and usually receive deference from their social inferiors. We can infer also that the moral outlook of the early nineteenth-century reader is markedly different from our own. Lydia's running away with Mr Wickham may surprise modern readers, given her extreme youth, but we are not likely to regard her adventure as necessarily leading to her complete social downfall unless it is dignified by marriage, nor as a stain of wickedness which will destroy her sisters' chances of marrying well.

SETTING

Austen writes with a careful sense of location – the reader always knows in what room of what house the action is taking place – but as with her characters, there is often surprisingly little detailed description. An exception to this is the guided tour round Pemberley and its park in Volume Three, Chapter I (Chapter 43), but of course this is to show exactly how wealthy and special Darcy is. There are three essential locations, in Hertfordshire, in Kent and in Derbyshire, and having a strong sense of these helps in mastering the plot. Events also take place in Brighton and London, but these happen 'off-stage', so to speak, and are reported by participants.

Meryton is a small town in Hertfordshire. It has a variety of shops and is big enough to hold the occasional 'public assembly'. The Bennets' house, called **Longbourn** after the village in which it is the main building, is one mile from Meryton. This is their only property; the Bennets do not have a winter residence in London. Three miles from Longbourn is **Netherfield Park**, rented by Mr Bingley; this distance is considered an easy walk for men and robust young women, notably Elizabeth, though Bingley usually makes the journey on horseback, as does Jane (in the rain). The Lucas and Philips families all live within walking distance of each other and the Bennets in the environs of Meryton.

Hunsford in Kent is the village of which Mr Collins is the vicar. The Parsonage shares one of its boundaries with **Rosings Park**, the magnificent home of Lady Catherine de Bourgh and her daughter Anne. In Volume Two, Chapter IX (Chapter 32), Elizabeth and Darcy disagree as to whether the fifty miles between Meryton and Hunsford is an 'easy distance' or not. For Darcy, 'fifty miles of good road' is 'little more than half a day's journey' (p. 174); Elizabeth points out that travel is expensive, and only the wealthy can consider such a distance easy.

Pemberley House in Derbyshire is a 'large, handsome, stone building' (p. 235), in a huge estate with its own woods and a river running through it. The park is ten miles round. Darcy spends about half the year there, the rest of the time in London. Five miles away is the village of **Lambton**, where Mrs Gardiner was brought up.

All the houses referred to above have their own land and gardens. Whenever the characters wish to be on their own, or to discuss matters privately, they find a suitable spot outside. Thus Elizabeth has her 'favourite haunt' (p. 178) in the park of Rosings, where Darcy finds her to hand over his letter. Lady Catherine, on her visit to Longbourn, chooses 'a prettyish kind of a little wilderness on one side of your lawn' (p. 333) as a suitably private spot in which to berate Elizabeth about her relationship with Darcy.

GRADE BOOSTER   A02

Examine Austen's use of locations in relation to her depiction of character.

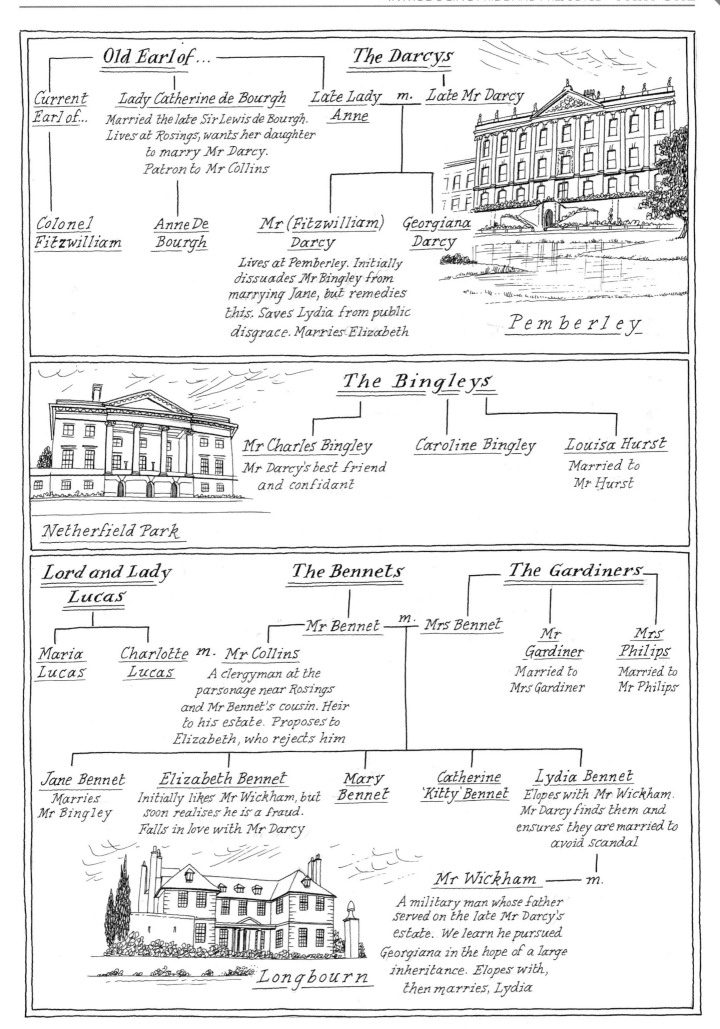

Old Earl of...

Current Earl of...

Lady Catherine de Bourgh
Married the late Sir Lewis de Bourgh. Lives at Rosings, wants her daughter to marry Mr Darcy. Patron to Mr Collins

The Darcys

Late Lady Anne — m. — Late Mr Darcy

Colonel Fitzwilliam

Anne De Bourgh

Mr (Fitzwilliam) Darcy
Lives at Pemberley. Initially dissuades Mr Bingley from marrying Jane, but remedies this. Saves Lydia from public disgrace. Marries Elizabeth

Georgiana Darcy

Pemberley

The Bingleys

Mr Charles Bingley
Mr Darcy's best friend and confidant

Caroline Bingley

Louisa Hurst
Married to Mr Hurst

Netherfield Park

Lord and Lady Lucas

Maria Lucas

Charlotte Lucas — m. — Mr Collins
A clergyman at the parsonage near Rosings and Mr Bennet's cousin. Heir to his estate. Proposes to Elizabeth, who rejects him

The Bennets

Mr Bennet — m. — Mrs Bennet

The Gardiners

Mr Gardiner
Married to Mrs Gardiner

Mrs Philips
Married to Mr Philips

Jane Bennet
Marries Mr Bingley

Elizabeth Bennet
Initially likes Mr Wickham, but soon realises he is a fraud. Falls in love with Mr Darcy

Mary Bennet

Catherine 'Kitty' Bennet

Lydia Bennet
Elopes with Mr Wickham. Mr Darcy finds them and ensures they are married to avoid scandal

Mr Wickham — m.
A military man whose father served on the late Mr Darcy's estate. We learn he pursued Georgiana in the hope of a large inheritance. Elopes with, then marries, Lydia

Longbourn

SYNOPSIS

VOLUME ONE

Mr and Mrs Bennet, of Longbourn near Meryton, have five daughters. Jane, the eldest, is beautiful and sensible. Next in age is Elizabeth, who is clever, witty and attractive. Neither Mrs Bennet nor her daughters can inherit their house because of a special law that dictates it must go to a male relative.

When a rich bachelor called Mr Bingley comes to stay at nearby Netherfield Park, he is drawn into the family circle as soon as possible. Mrs Bennet devises stratagems to bring the young people together. Jane falls in love with Bingley, and Bingley seems to return Jane's love. Elizabeth takes a strong dislike to Mr Darcy, Bingley's friend, who is wealthy but proud.

The militia comes to Meryton and the two youngest Bennet girls, Kitty and Lydia, flirt with the officers. Elizabeth is charmed by a newcomer called Mr Wickham. Wickham grew up with Darcy, but detests him as he believes Darcy cruelly deprived him of a career in the church.

Bingley suddenly departs for London, leaving Jane miserable. Meanwhile Mr Collins, who will inherit their house, comes to visit the Bennets. He is a disagreeably pompous clergyman and has decided to marry one of the Bennet sisters. He proposes to Elizabeth, who refuses him. He successfully turns his attentions to Charlotte Lucas, Elizabeth's friend.

CONTEXT **A03**

'Three-decker' (three-volume) novels were a standard publishing format for long fictions during the nineteenth century.

VOLUME TWO

Jane goes to stay in London with her aunt and uncle, Mr and Mrs Gardiner, hoping to see Bingley. Elizabeth goes to stay with Charlotte Collins in Kent. Bingley's sister Caroline, who had been so friendly to Jane in Meryton, is now cold and distant. Elizabeth believes that Darcy's snobbery is responsible for separating Jane and Bingley.

In Kent Elizabeth again meets Darcy, who is staying with his aunt, Lady Catherine de Bourgh. Darcy proposes marriage to Elizabeth. Tactlessly, he emphasises the vulgarity of Elizabeth's family in the midst of his proud declaration of love. She angrily refuses him.

In a letter to Elizabeth, Darcy justifies making Bingley stop seeing Jane: he thought she was not in love. He also spells out the true history of Wickham, who is in fact a spendthrift and a seducer. Darcy's young sister Georgiana has been a victim of Wickham's false charm.

Back at Longbourn, Elizabeth disapproves of Lydia's going to stay in Brighton, where the militia's new camp is located.

VOLUME THREE

Elizabeth goes on a holiday tour with the Gardiners. They visit Pemberley, Darcy's impressive country estate. To her embarrassment Darcy unexpectedly turns up. He is astonishingly kind to her. Then bad news arrives: Lydia has run away with Wickham.

Elizabeth rushes back to Longbourn. Mr Gardiner goes to help her father try to find the fugitives in London. A deal is made with Wickham to make him marry Lydia. Lydia and Wickham visit the family and are unashamed of their behaviour.

Elizabeth learns from Mrs Gardiner that it was Darcy who helped to find Wickham and provided the money to make him marry Lydia. Bingley moves back to Netherfield, courts Jane, and proposes. Darcy has accompanied him, and also visits the Bennets, but seems less keen on Elizabeth than he was at Pemberley. Lady Catherine makes a surprise visit. She is intent on preventing Elizabeth's marriage to her nephew Darcy, of which she has heard rumours.

Elizabeth grasps an opportunity to thank Darcy for his secret activities on behalf of Lydia. He proposes to her again and is accepted.

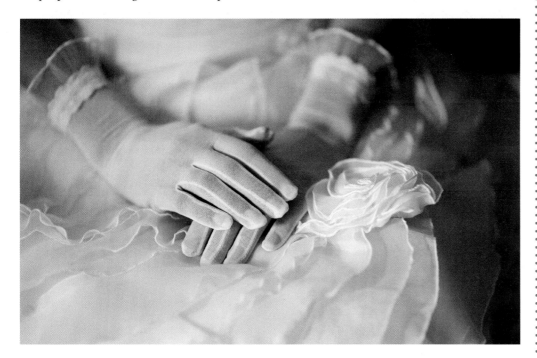

CHECK THE FILM **A03**

The excellent BBC adaptation of the novel by Andrew Davies (1995), starring Jennifer Ehle as Elizabeth Bennet and Colin Firth as Darcy, is easily available and will be referred to throughout these Notes, as a foil for and a contrast to the novel itself. It is by no means an exact adaptation, and incorporates many new scenes and dialogues, which may be memorable and effective in their own right. It should not be seen as a substitute for reading the novel, as it offers a quite different experience.

CONTEXT **A04**

The main characters in the novel are the elite leisured class. At the time the novel was written, novel-reading relied on a degree of leisure that was not available to most people and so it is likely that the readers Jane Austen had in mind for her novel were of a class not dissimilar to that of her characters.

VOLUME ONE, CHAPTER I (CHAPTER 1)

SUMMARY

- The author introduces as a 'truth' that a man who is single and 'in possession of a good fortune' will be 'in want of a wife' (p. 5).
- Mr Bennet is encouraged by his wife to visit Mr Bingley, the new tenant of Netherfield Park, who is both single and rich.
- Mrs Bennet hopes that Mr Bingley can be prevailed upon to marry one of her five daughters. She begs her husband to arrange a visit.
- Mr Bennet teases his wife and appears to refuse her request.
- The author summarises the Bennets' characteristics and emphasises Mrs Bennet's mission 'to get her daughters married' (p. 7).

ANALYSIS

THE 'TRUTH' ABOUT CHARACTER

This first chapter introduces the moral framework of the novel as a whole. What are the values Mr and Mrs Bennet attribute to their daughters? Jane is handsome; Lydia is good-humoured. Mr Bennet dismisses them all as 'silly and ignorant, like other girls' (p. 6), but commends Lizzy for her 'quickness' (p. 6). What are the values that we as readers are asked to bring to bear on the Bennets? Mr Bennet stands back from his wife, and quietly enjoys his superiority through his teasing mockery. We as readers have to do the same since the text forces us to adopt Mr Bennet's and the **narrator**'s **ironic** stance. In case we have missed the point, the narrator finally tells us what to think of them: 'Mr Bennet was so odd a mixture of quick parts … *Her* mind was less difficult to develop' (p. 7). Indeed Mrs Bennet is presented as someone with a poor understanding of her husband's character and little self-knowledge. From the very beginning, Austen places in the **foreground** of her novel the importance of understanding character – and the ease with which a person's character can be misread and misunderstood.

AUTHORIAL VIEWPOINT

The first and last paragraphs of the chapter have a special **register** and perspective, sandwiching Mr and Mrs Bennet's **dialogue** that takes up most of the chapter. The chapter ends as it began: with a paragraph of **authorial intervention**. Austen describes Mr and Mrs Bennet's characteristics in a series of direct and pithy sentences. The reader is perhaps a little surprised by the severity with which Mrs Bennet is summed up ('mean understanding, little information, and uncertain temper', p. 7).

STUDY FOCUS: MARRIAGE AND MONEY A04

The themes of marriage and money are inextricably linked from the very first sentence of Austen's novel. The income of prospective suitors for any of her daughters' hands in marriage is a matter of importance for Mrs Bennet, and Mr Bennet teases her about this: 'But I hope you will get over it, and live to see many young men of four thousand a year come into the neighbourhood' (p. 7).

When Mrs Bennet married Mr Bennet, she would have brought with her a marriage settlement or dowry from her own family, money that would have been spent – little by little – on her own and her daughters' clothes and similar items. Mr Bennet is a landowner but not a particularly wealthy one; moreover, as the father of five daughters and no sons, he has no male heir.

Austen uses humour to draw attention to the importance of making a good match. Such is the interest in a potential suitor entering the neighbourhood that 'he is considered as the rightful property of some one or other of their daughters' (p. 5). Perhaps it is no wonder that, with five daughters to marry off, Mrs Bennet thrives on 'visiting and news' (p. 7).

CRITICAL VIEWPOINT A03

Mrs Bennet has commonly been regarded by critics as 'one of the more absurd and comic figures of English fiction'. As you read the novel, consider to what extent you consider this a suitable description of her words and actions.

KEY QUOTATION: VOLUME ONE, CHAPTER I (1) A01

Key quotation: 'It is a truth universally acknowledged, that a single man in possession of a good fortune, must be in want of a wife' (p. 5).

- This opening sentence reads like an **aphorism**. The tone is rather grand, detached and knowing. However, the subject matter may seem rather small and frivolous by comparison!

- Austen provides an introduction to and ironic statement about the **themes** of the novel. The topics of money and marriage ('fortune' and 'wife') are introduced in relation to 'truth' and who should acknowledge it.

- The author has immediately focused the reader's attention on one provincial neighbourhood and its families, and the need to marry off daughters as well as possible.

- We must be on our guard not to be taken in by the narrator's playfully ironic approach.

GLOSSARY

5	**a chaise and four** a horse-drawn carriage
5	**Michaelmas** a date in the Christian calendar (29 September) in honour of Archangel Michael
7	**caprice** whim or impulse

VOLUME ONE, CHAPTER II (CHAPTER 2)

SUMMARY

- We discover that Mr Bennet was one of the first to visit Mr Bingley at Netherfield Park.
- We also learn that Mr Bennet had always intended to visit him but that he chose to tease his family on the subject.
- On hearing about the visit the following evening, Mrs Bennet is in raptures, praises her husband (while taking some of the credit for his achievement) and imagines her youngest daughter, Lydia, dancing with Bingley.
- After Mr Bennet has left the room, the women speculate about when Mr Bingley will call on them.

ANALYSIS

THE BENNET DAUGHTERS

In this chapter, we meet some of the Bennet daughters for the first time. Elizabeth's views on paying Mr Bingley a visit show her to be more measured and reasonable than her mother: 'But you forget … that we shall meet him at the assemblies, and that Mrs Long has promised to introduce him' (p. 8). Poor Kitty is scolded by Mrs Bennet for coughing. Mary's seriousness is the butt of her father's **ironic** humour. She 'read[s] great books, and make[s] extracts' (p. 9), but Austen hints that she is neither witty nor clever: 'Mary wished to say something very sensible, but knew not how' (p. 9).

Except for what we are told by the author at the start and finish of this chapter, most of the chapter is written in **dialogue**. So, rather like a theatre audience, we base our first impressions of the characters on what they say and do rather than on what the **narrator** tells us about them.

STUDY FOCUS: CONTRASTING REACTIONS   A02

The **comic tone** of the preceding chapter continues in Chapter II (Chapter 2). The reader is told of Mr Bennet's deliberate concealment of his actions and can enjoy the comedy that arises from his equally deliberate misinterpretation of his wife's comments. There is also comedy in the contrast between Mrs Bennet's tetchy and resentful mood at the beginning of the chapter and her 'tumult of joy' (p. 9) once she discovers the news that the visit to Mr Bingley has taken place.

By showing us different reactions to this situation, Austen is developing and deepening our understanding of some of the novel's main characters. Similar examples of this method of **characterisation** can be found in Chapter V (Chapter 5), in which pride is the subject of discussion, and Chapter XIII (Chapter 13), where a variety of responses to Mr Collins's letter are depicted.

GRADE BOOSTER   A02

Take notes from this chapter and elsewhere in the novel about what we learn and infer about the lives of young women at this time: about typical activities and pastimes, for example. How does your evidence compare with what you learn about the lives of the young men we encounter?

CRITICAL VIEWPOINT   A04

Mr Bennet deals with his family here in an ironic and teasing way. Do you find this to be amusing or cruel behaviour?

GLOSSARY

8	**assemblies**	public balls
9	**circumspection**	caution, good judgement
9	**make extracts**	copy passages from one's reading into a book
10	**conjecturing**	expressing opinions or making judgements based on guesswork

VOLUME ONE, CHAPTER III (CHAPTER 3)

SUMMARY

- Bingley repays Mr Bennet's visit but the Bennet daughters only catch a glimpse of him.

- Bingley cannot come to dinner with the Bennets because he must go to London. Rumour has it that he will attend the forthcoming ball at Meryton with a large party of twelve ladies and seven gentlemen.

- The ball takes place and Bingley's party is of five people: Bingley himself, his two sisters, one with a husband, and one other man – a Mr Darcy. News of Darcy's wealth (ten thousand pounds a year) spreads rapidly around the ballroom.

- Bingley dances twice with Jane Bennet, while his friend Darcy is discovered to be proud and haughty, choosing to dance only with Bingley's sisters and snubbing Elizabeth.

- Mrs Bennet and her daughters give an impatient Mr Bennet a detailed account of the ball.

ANALYSIS

FIRST IMPRESSIONS OF BINGLEY

Mr Bennet refuses to give his family a satisfactory description of Bingley. However, their neighbours Sir William and Lady Lucas describe him as 'quite young, wonderfully handsome, extremely agreeable' (p. 11) and everyone is pleased that he plans to attend the next social gathering with a large party, suggesting that he is sociable, popular and well connected.

The visit has been returned, but Bingley does not meet the Bennet daughters, who spy on him from an upstairs window from where they observe that he 'wore a blue coat and rode a black horse' (p. 11). Their spying on Bingley and fascination with even the smallest details about him leaves both the sisters and the reader intrigued to see more of Bingley and builds excitement about the ball. Interest in this character continues to run high.

STUDY FOCUS: DANCING PARTNERS A02

Bingley and Darcy are established as contrasting characters. Darcy's pride connects him directly with the novel's title. Again, we see how quickly opinions of people can change; Mrs Bennet seems to judge people only by their clothes and appearance, until Darcy's sour manners and poor dancing etiquette give her a much less favourable opinion of him. Earlier in the chapter, the narrator states that 'To be fond of dancing was a certain step towards falling in love'(p. 11). We can see that the desire to dance is being used by Austen to give us insights into characters' openness and amiability.

We see Bingley and Jane Bennet paired, and when Elizabeth sits out for two dances we are encouraged to see Elizabeth and Darcy as a potential pairing. But when Elizabeth and Darcy do not dance together, we as readers are invited to suppose that things are not going to go smoothly for them – either on or off the dance floor.

CONTEXT A04

The ball takes place in an assembly room; it is a public entertainment, in relatively modest circumstances, unlike Bingley's more magnificent ball at Netherfield in Chapter XVIII (Chapter 18). Dancing is a common **motif** in Austen's novels; it allows men and women to interact with each other physically and in conversation. Jane Austen herself loved dancing.

GRADE BOOSTER A02

Read again the dialogue between Bingley and Darcy that Elizabeth overhears. What do we learn about Darcy's character during this short private conversation? What does Elizabeth's reaction show us of her character?

CRITICAL VIEWPOINT A04

In the 1995 BBC adaptation of the novel, viewers are shown drunken yokels frolicking in the street outside the assembly hall – not the kind of scene that occurs anywhere in the novel. Why do you think this scene was added?

GLOSSARY

| 12 | **mein** a person's look or manner (usually spelt 'mien') |
| 15 | **Boulanger** a lively dance |

VOLUME ONE, CHAPTER IV (CHAPTER 4)

SUMMARY

- Jane and Elizabeth discuss Bingley, and then his sisters. Elizabeth thinks them conceited while Jane is determined to think well of everyone.
- We learn more about Bingley's financial situation.
- Bingley and Darcy are compared, and so are Jane and Elizabeth.

ANALYSIS

CONTRASTING CHARACTERS: BINGLEY AND DARCY

The characters of Bingley and Darcy are opposed. Bingley is easy-going and amiable and trusts his friend's judgement entirely, while Darcy is cleverer but 'haughty' and 'reserved' (p. 18). Bingley's character brings him popularity while Darcy is likely to give offence. However a close and 'steady friendship' (p. 18) clearly exists between the two men.

CONTRASTING CHARACTERS: JANE AND ELIZABETH

We are shown that Jane is serious and gentle and sees the best in everyone. Elizabeth lovingly counsels her that she is 'too apt you know, to like people in general' (p. 16). The Bingley sisters describe her as 'sweet' (p. 18). Elizabeth meanwhile combines deep respect and love for her sister with a playful sense of humour. She shares her father's taste for **irony**: a young man, she remarks, must be handsome 'if he possibly can' (p. 16).

Her humorous comments may remind us not only of her father but also of Austen's authorial comments and summaries. Austen is using Elizabeth as a **centre of consciousness**. She is not the **narrator** of *Pride and Prejudice* but as readers we may often feel we are seeing events through her eyes. Indeed, according to the narrator, Elizabeth has 'more quickness of observation and less pliancy of temper than her sister' (p. 17), qualities which recommend her to the reader as a perceptive judge of character.

STUDY FOCUS: MONEY AND CLASS

We note that Bingley's money comes from 'trade', and that his family are recent arrivals in the landed gentry. Furthermore, Bingley is only the tenant of Netherfield so does not yet own an estate. His sisters, we are told, are 'very anxious for his having an estate of his own' (p. 17) and it is strongly suggested that the way by which the family attained their wealth is something they do not dwell on, for fear of appearing less 'respectable' (p. 17).

The contempt that those with 'estates' may feel towards others who have to work for their living is shown on several occasions throughout the book, notably in occasional comments by Caroline Bingley. In this chapter, the Bingley sisters' fortune of twenty thousand pounds, and 'habits of spending more than they ought, and of associating with people of rank' (p. 17) have translated into their 'think[ing] well of themselves, and meanly of others' (p. 17). This could be seen as showing their lack of security in a society where social mobility is not uncommon.

GLOSSARY

16 **candour** meant 'purity; integrity; freedom from bias or malice' in Austen's time, rather that its present day meaning of 'frankness; outspokenness'

18 **Miss Bennet** the oldest daughter has the right to be called Miss Bennet; the others are Miss Elizabeth Bennet, Miss Mary Bennet, etc.

VOLUME ONE, CHAPTER V (CHAPTER 5)

SUMMARY

- We learn about Sir William Lucas who prospered in trade, received his knighthood and retired in search of a respectable country life appropriate to his new social standing.
- The Lucas family visit the Bennets and discuss the ball. Mrs Bennet remains delighted that Bingley appeared to favour Jane at the ball.
- Darcy is criticised, and Jane, believing good of everyone, tries to moderate the complaints.
- Mary Bennet sermonises in a boring way on the nature of pride and vanity.

ANALYSIS

TALKING OVER THE BALL

The Lucases live very near the Bennets and the eldest daughter, Charlotte, is a particular friend of Elizabeth's. Indeed, we are shown that the two families frequently socialise and are reminded of the importance of the ball in both families' social calendar: 'That the Miss Lucases and the Miss Bennets should meet to talk over a ball was absolutely necessary' (p. 19).

During the discussion, Mrs Bennet betrays how much she is jumping to conclusions about the future of Bingley's admiration for Jane, while simultaneously denying that she is doing so: 'that does seem as if – but however, it may all come to nothing you know' (p. 20). Her incoherence here – characterised by short phrases and a plentiful use of dashes in her passages of speech – is in sharp contrast with the verbal powers of the narrator, and of more intelligent characters such as Elizabeth.

STUDY FOCUS: PRIDE — A02

Pride, one of the explicit **themes** of the novel, is discussed here in various ways. The introductory summary of Sir William Lucas is a masterpiece of ironic portraiture. The narrator tells us that his knighthood affected him adversely, that 'The distinction had perhaps been felt too strongly' and that he had been left with 'a disgust to his business and to his residence in a small market town' (p. 19). He is, however, a friendly, obliging and courteous character. Here Austen adds some depth and complexity to what seemed to begin as a **satiric caricature**.

Pride is again explicitly mentioned in reference to Darcy. Opinions vary, however: while Mrs Bennet is unreserved in her criticism of his proud and snobbish nature, Jane typically speaks up to defend the man, and Charlotte Lucas excuses his pride, saying, 'One cannot wonder that so very fine a young man, with family, fortune, every thing in his favour, should think highly of himself' (p. 21). Might she be thinking of her own father here?

Mary's thoughts also turn to the theme of pride, but unlike the others she speaks in a serious tone and in generalities. The mood is lifted by a Lucas boy's exclamation that 'If I were as rich as Mr Darcy ... I should not care how proud I was' (p. 21). The entrance of wealthy gentlemen into the social milieu of the Bennets and the Lucases continues to lead to much enthusiastic discussion and speculation about the new arrivals' characters and behaviour.

GRADE BOOSTER A02

What are your first impressions of Elizabeth's good friend Charlotte Lucas? What does the reader learn about her circumstances, her prospects and her general outlook on life?

CRITICAL VIEWPOINT A04

Many modern works borrow from earlier texts (**intertextuality**). The film *Bride and Prejudice* (2004) takes its plot almost entirely from the novel. Other recent examples include Seth Grahame-Smith's novel *Pride and Prejudice and Zombies* (2009) and the British TV series *Lost in Austen* (2008). Find out about how some contemporary film-makers, bloggers, novelists and others have been inspired by and have borrowed from *Pride and Prejudice*.

GLOSSARY

19 **St James's** St James's Palace in Pall Mall was the royal residence until Queen Victoria moved into Buckingham Palace in 1837

20 **hack chaise** a hired carriage, denoting a relative lack of wealth

VOLUME ONE, CHAPTER VI (CHAPTER 6)

SUMMARY

- The Bennet women visit Netherfield, and Bingley's sisters repay the visit. Elizabeth still does not like them, but they are kind to Jane. This is proof, Elizabeth thinks, of Bingley's interest in Jane.
- Elizabeth and Charlotte Lucas discuss courtship and marriage and, in particular, how Jane should behave towards Bingley.
- Darcy has started to change his mind about Elizabeth. At a party at the Lucas household, Sir William discusses dancing with Darcy and tries to persuade him to dance with Elizabeth, who makes her excuses.
- Miss Bingley sidles over to Darcy and expresses her disgust at the evening. When Darcy reveals to Miss Bingley that he is attracted to Elizabeth, she teases him about an imagined marriage and his prospective mother-in-law.

ANALYSIS

FALLING IN LOVE

Jane is falling in love, but such is her 'composure of temper and … uniform cheerfulness of manner' (p. 22) that only those who know her well would realise.

Charlotte Lucas suggests that Jane is too guarded and self-controlled and that she risks losing Bingley by not encouraging him more openly. Elizabeth defends Jane's modesty.

The narrator's focus then moves to Darcy, whose pride and prejudice are being subtly undone by 'a pair of fine eyes in the face of a pretty woman' (p. 27). Austen combines insights from the **omniscient narrator** about Darcy's changed feelings with dramatised **dialogue** left for the reader to interpret, though hints abound. We are told that Mr Darcy approaches Elizabeth and Charlotte 'though without seeming to have any intention of speaking' (p. 25), whereupon Elizabeth teases him about his listening in on her conversation with Colonel Forster. Elizabeth's dialogue here is characteristically robust and quick-witted.

Later, Sir William Lucas entreats Darcy and Elizabeth to dance with each other but here Elizabeth's dialogue shows her 'discomposure' and archness as she sarcastically – but smilingly – suggests that Darcy would dance with her only out of 'politeness' (p. 27). Elizabeth, spurned at the first dance, is now filled with wounded pride and prejudice against him. Such misalignment of views has much comic potential.

At the end of the chapter, the narrator draws attention to Darcy's 'great intrepidity' (p. 28) in revealing Elizabeth as the subject of his meditations. His revelation results in Miss Bingley's impertinent teasing. Again, Austen is making us consider whether it is better to be guarded about one's feelings or to openly display them.

STUDY FOCUS: COURTSHIP AND MARRIAGE   A02

Austen clearly wishes to debate what is the appropriate behaviour of young women who are on the brink of courtship. How soon should they allow themselves to give way to and give away their feelings? How much should they leave their suitors to make the running, and how much should they lead them on? The unfolding of the **plot** will show whether either Charlotte or Elizabeth is correct.

Charlotte Lucas's pessimistic, non-romantic and even cynical attitude to the chance of happiness in marriage requires attention: a 'share of vexation' (p. 24) seems unavoidable in wedlock, however well the parties might know each other. Elizabeth laughs off this view as 'not sound' (p. 24), suggesting that she has a more positive view of Charlotte's nature – 'you would never act in this way yourself' (p. 24) – and of human nature in general.

KEY QUOTATIONS: VOLUME ONE, CHAPTER VI (CHAPTER 6)   A01

Key quotation: 'Though he had detected with a critical eye more than one failure of perfect symmetry in her form, he was forced to acknowledge her figure to be light and pleasing; and in spite of his asserting that her manners were not those of the fashionable world, he was caught by their easy playfulness' (p. 24).

- In spite of all his adverse judgements about her beauty and personality, Darcy is drawn to admire Elizabeth.

- Phrases such as 'critical eye', 'failure', 'forced' and 'caught' give the reader the impression that Darcy's feelings have now got the better of him.

- The passage directly contradicts Darcy's assessment of Elizabeth at the ball in Chapter III (Chapter 3).

GLOSSARY	
23	**Vingt-un and Commerce** card games
27	**complaisance and complacency** desire to please and quiet satisfaction

REVISION FOCUS: TASK 1   A03

How far do you agree with the following statements?

- Austen, like Darcy, has 'a very satirical eye' (p. 25).
- Charlotte's views on love, courtship and marriage are of vital importance for the novel as a whole.

Write opening paragraphs for essays based on these discussion points. Set out your arguments clearly.

VOLUME ONE, CHAPTER VII (CHAPTER 7)

SUMMARY

- The Bennets' financial and social standing is described. Mr Bennet's property brings him two thousand pounds a year, but on his death both his estate and this income will be inherited by a distant male relative.
- Catherine and Lydia often walk to Meryton to see their aunt and to find out more about the militia regiment that has recently moved into the neighbourhood.
- Jane is invited to Netherfield. Mrs Bennet insists that Jane go by horseback, in the hope that she will be unable to return home because of the impending rain. Jane catches a cold and has to stay there.
- Elizabeth decides to walk the three miles to see her sister. Jane is ill, but overjoyed to see Elizabeth. In the afternoon Elizabeth is invited to stay at Netherfield.

ANALYSIS

THE MILITIA

Catherine and Lydia are excited that a regiment of militia has taken up headquarters in the town. Their aunt, Mrs Philips, introduces them to the officers, and they are obsessed by this new society: 'They could talk of nothing but officers' (p. 30). For Catherine and Lydia, even the topic of Mr Bingley's fortune is now of secondary interest 'when opposed to the regimentals of an ensign' (p. 30).

Predictably, the young ladies' parents react differently to Catherine and Lydia's 'effusions on this subject' (p. 30). Mr Bennet accuses them of being 'the silliest girls in the country' and 'uncommonly foolish' (p. 30). Mrs Bennet, however, defends them, citing her own former fondness for a 'red-coat' (p. 30). As ever, she has marriage on her mind, and hopes to find an eligible colonel 'with five or six thousand a year' (p. 30) for one of her daughters.

FORTUNE AND MARRIAGE

Austen is precise and detailed in exposing the incomes of her various characters, and the means by which their wealth has been procured. Each male character (and here Mrs Bennet too) is placed exactly according to a scale of money and respectability. As anticipated in the first sentence of the novel, the **themes** of fortune and marriage are linked; we see Mrs Bennet putting a price on Lydia and Catherine, and risking Jane's health in order to thrust her into Bingley's company.

STUDY FOCUS: AUSTEN'S USE OF IRONY A02

A good example of Austen's **irony**, where she says quite the opposite of what she means, is to be found in her icy condemnation of Mrs Bennet's plan, and its unfortunate outcome for Jane who is made ill by the soaking she receives. Austen tells us that Jane's sisters 'were uneasy for her, but her mother was delighted' (p. 32) and Mrs Bennet is clearly proud of her scheme: 'This was a lucky idea of mine, indeed!' (p. 32).

Austen leads the reader to share in the other family members' misgivings about Jane riding to Netherfield in a downpour; when Austen writes that 'Till the next morning, however, she was not aware of all the felicity of her contrivance' (p. 32), the reader recognises that the word 'felicity' is being used ironically and that the news from Jane will be far from happy. Mrs Bennet is thus seen here as at best sillier than her silliest daughters and at worst somewhat ruthless and mercenary.

VOLUME ONE, CHAPTERS VIII AND IX (CHAPTERS 8 AND 9)

SUMMARY

- Jane's health has not improved and Bingley is clearly anxious about her.
- Miss Bingley mocks Elizabeth's behaviour and family.
- Darcy's estate at Pemberley, his library and his sister are described and the ideal qualities of an accomplished woman are discussed. Darcy remarks that he dislikes female cunning employed for 'captivation' (p. 36), to Miss Bingley's discomfort.
- Jane's health improves a little. Mrs Bennet visits Netherfield, declares Jane unfit to return home and embarrasses Elizabeth.
- Bingley agrees to organise a ball and sets the date for after Jane's recovery.

ANALYSIS

ELIZABETH'S APPEARANCE AND RELATIONS

When Elizabeth leaves the room after dinner in Chapter VIII (Chapter 8), Miss Bingley criticises her appearance and her manners. Mrs Hurst comments adversely on how 'wild' (p. 36) Elizabeth looked after the walk and they mock her dirty petticoat. Miss Bingley tries to involve Darcy in the dispraise of Elizabeth but with little success (which may remind the reader of Darcy's 'admiration of the brilliancy which exercise had given to her complexion' in Chapter VII (Chapter 7), when Elizabeth first arrives at Netherfield).

The vulgarity of the Bennets' relations are a further source of laughter between the two sisters, despite their declared regard for Jane: 'his sisters … indulged their mirth for some time at the expense of their dear friend's vulgar relations' (p. 37). This suggests that the sisters can be spiteful and hypocritical in their treatment of others.

READING HABITS

In the evening Elizabeth chooses not to join the rest of the party at cards. Her preference for reading a book causes surprise: 'that is rather singular' (p. 37), declares Mr Hurst. Austen uses the discussion about libraries that follows to establish the difference between Darcy and Bingley. The latter is portrayed as something of an upstart with no great love of reading and a meagre library, a result of his family's recently acquired wealth. Darcy's library has been the work of generations and of his own passion for reading: 'I cannot comprehend the neglect of a family library in such days as these' (p. 38). Reading and books, like dancing and money, are **motifs** which reappear in the novel (see Chapters XI and XII (Chapters 11 and 12)). Interestingly, Mr Bennet has an extensive library and is an avid reader ('With a book he was regardless of time', Chapter III (Chapter 3)).

STUDY FOCUS: A COMEDY OF CHARACTERS | A02

Austen handles the complications of the gathering in Chapter IX (Chapter 9) when Mrs Bennet visits Netherfield with consummate skill. Every comment and nuance adds to our understanding of the characters' feelings and attitudes. Indeed, the chapter opens with a conversation between Bingley and Elizabeth about the very business of being 'a studier of character' (p. 42). The contrasts between characters' understandings and motivations, and the awkwardness and embarrassment that ensue, are typical of **social comedy**.

GRADE BOOSTER | A02

Lydia is described for the first time in this chapter. Make notes about what we learn about her and add to them as we learn more about each of the sisters.

CONTEXT | A03

Austen's own novels would have been available in the public lending libraries that were becoming more common during this period.

GLOSSARY

37 **at loo** playing a card game

VOLUME ONE, CHAPTERS X AND XI (CHAPTERS 10 AND 11)

SUMMARY

- During an evening at Netherfield, Miss Bingley attempts to win Darcy's attention while he is writing a letter to his sister but fails.
- Bingley's and Darcy's letter-writing styles are compared and a friendly but serious discussion about Bingley's yielding nature and susceptibility to the influence of others ensues, in which Elizabeth holds her own.
- Elizabeth notices that Darcy is continually observing her and wonders what she is doing wrong to attract his notice. She does not imagine he could be admiring her.
- Miss Bingley tries to provoke Darcy by talking about his supposed marriage with Elizabeth, and behaves rudely towards Elizabeth on a walk.
- Jane's health takes a turn for the better and Elizabeth is pleased to see how attentive and caring Bingley is towards her sister.
- Darcy's interest in Elizabeth increases, which piques Miss Bingley's jealousy. Elizabeth and Darcy discuss whether he is faultless.

ANALYSIS

DARCY AND ELIZABETH

Darcy appreciates the 'danger of paying Elizabeth too much attention' (p. 51), an echo of the observation in Chapter X (Chapter 10) that 'if it were not for the inferiority of her connections, he should be in some danger'. Austen shows the reader that Darcy is very much aware how careful he must be in the choice of a wife. We have also seen that Darcy is a proud man and in Chapter XI (Chapter 11) he describes himself as 'too little yielding' (p. 56), yet his feelings for Elizabeth have triumphed over any counter-arguments.

In Chapter XI (Chapter 11), we see the pair verbally sparring, proof that they are well matched in intelligence and quick-wittedness. Elizabeth **ironically** concludes that Darcy is too perfect to be laughed at while Darcy ventures that he is rightly and not excessively proud – 'where there is a real superiority of mind, pride will always be under good regulation' (p. 56) – and admits that he bears grudges. Elizabeth accuses him of hating everybody, and he accuses her of wilfully misunderstanding them.

STUDY FOCUS: CAROLINE BINGLEY **A02**

Drawing room conversation takes up a large part of Chapters X and XI (Chapters 10 and 11). Caroline Bingley's attempts to win Darcy's attentions for herself are becoming more desperate. In Chapter X (Chapter 10) she regularly interrupts his letter-writing and in Chapter XI (Chapter 11) she attempts to interrupt his reading, but it is to no avail. It is only when Elizabeth joins the conversation on page 55 that Darcy, a moment ago 'inflexibly studious', becomes instantly interested.

In Chapter X (Chapter 10), Caroline is described as trying 'to provoke Darcy into disliking her guest' (p. 51) by listing what she perceives as her character flaws and unfavourable background. Once again we see her snobbery but also her energy and persistence in trying to win Darcy's attention and affection. She thinks nothing of choosing a book purely because it is the second volume of the one he is reading, and earlier we hear that she 'had obtained private intelligence that Mr Darcy did not wish for cards' (p. 53). The author uses telling details such as these to build a gradual impression of Caroline Bingley's scheming ways.

GRADE BOOSTER **A02**

How do these chapters contribute to the novel's exploration of the themes of 'pride' and 'prejudice'?

CRITICAL VIEWPOINT **A04**

It is possible that *Pride and Prejudice* was originally conceived as an **epistolary novel**, and there are many letters in the finished version. The literary critic Tony Tanner describes a letter as 'a transforming of action into words which may then be reflected on in a way which is impossible when one is actually involved in the action'. As you read on, think about the role letter-writing plays in terms of plot and character development.

GLOSSARY

46   **piquet** a complicated card game

48   **panegyric** a speech in praise of a person or thing

EXTENDED COMMENTARY

VOLUME ONE, CHAPTER XI (CHAPTER 11), PP. 56–7

Elizabeth Bennet is celebrated as a character for her lively wit and independence of mind, and this passage provides evidence for such a view. Here, she is at Netherfield, where she is looking after her sister Jane. It is the evening of the second day spent there,  so she is already familiar with the company. This is the last of several conversations which she and Darcy have covering a variety of topics, including reading, letter-writing, the pliancy of Bingley as a friend, and desirable accomplishments for young women. As in most of these discussions, she and Darcy become sparring partners to the exclusion of the others, in this case Caroline Bingley. Caroline is beginning to feel that Elizabeth is interesting to Darcy, though he has not yet admitted to admiring her 'fine eyes' (p. 27), so Caroline's jealousy is still emerging, rather than full-blown. Darcy himself has stung Elizabeth by calling her only 'tolerable' (p. 13) and, within the bounds of politeness, she is out to avenge this insult. Her assertion, therefore, that Darcy is beyond laughter is something of a taunt. Her comment is in answer to Caroline's refusal to tease Darcy: 'Teaze calmness of temper and presence of mind. No, no … ' (p. 56).

CONTEXT A04

'Temper' as used by Darcy here means 'temperament'.

This is a little drama of sexual attraction, which seems to be on everyone's mind whether they experience it or not. Austen captures the way Caroline does all she can to praise Darcy, and does not interest him, while Elizabeth does all she can to annoy him, and thereby is attractive to him. It is this rivalry between the two young women, deeply felt by Caroline, but entered into light-heartedly by Elizabeth, that is the **subtext** of the early discussion. Now the subtext changes as Elizabeth brings her wit to bear on Darcy, whose pride has so annoyed her. Caroline is left out of the conversation – she eventually brings it to an end, piqued that things have got out of her control.

The subject of their exchange is of central interest in *Pride and Prejudice*. Who and what have we the right to laugh at? The novel adopts an ironic and **satiric** attitude to much of its material. Here the propriety of such a way of viewing things is discussed. Elizabeth asserts that it is uncommon for anyone to be laughter-proof. It is mildly **paradoxical** that she wants acquaintances that she can laugh at, as if she wants fools for friends. The implication is that everyone, even the present company, can be the butt of derision. Darcy replies with some gravity that anyone can be made to look ridiculous by a frivolous-minded person, by implication like Elizabeth. She offers a conventional defence of satire – hers is aimed only at human folly and she will never mock the wise and good. We may speculate that this is also the **narrator**'s position. Then Elizabeth turns the conversation back against Darcy, by drawing from his comment the false conclusion that he is without fault. His reply, that he attempts to avoid weakness, is rather pompous and feeble, and he emphasises his good qualities, his 'study' and his 'strong understanding'. Elizabeth delivers her *coup de grâce* (her final blow): 'vanity and pride' is what she detests in Darcy and the present company. Given the title of the novel, the reader is alert to the implications of this attack. An explicit **theme** of the book, already broached in a number of preceding chapters (see Mary's homily and Charlotte's comment in Chapter V (Chapter 5)), is under discussion.

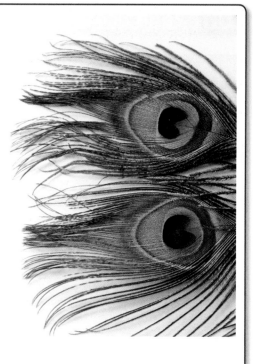

CHECK THE BOOK   **A04**

Mary Wollstonecraft (1759–97) is known as one of the first modern English feminist writers and intellectuals. In 1790 she wrote that 'Civilised women … are weakened by false refinement … All their thoughts turn on things calculated to excite emotion and feeling, when they should reason.' Elizabeth is frequently shown, as she is here, to be an intelligent woman with a talent for reasoning and wit.

Darcy pronounces on his sense of superiority in the following grave terms: 'vanity is a weakness indeed. But pride – where there is a real superiority of mind, pride will be always under good regulation.' He seems to change his mind in mid-sentence. The natural sequence of ideas after the 'but' is to say that pride is not a weakness: vanity is, but pride isn't. Alert to the trap she has laid, he states instead that it requires to be properly controlled. Indeed, his answer shows exactly such proper control. Elizabeth has to hide her triumph and amusement. She has found a way of attacking his vice.

Darcy seems to know he is under attack, and his only defence is a reasonable seriousness; but it makes him sound pompous in contrast with Elizabeth's lightness of thrust. But then he further traps himself in her conversational sparring by admitting to being 'resentful'. So now Elizabeth can chide him with the fault of 'implacable resentment', then exaggerated into 'a propensity to hate every body'. She has indeed found a 'shade' in his character. His riposte gracefully admits defeat.

Elizabeth is shown irrepressibly teasing Darcy's seriousness and self-importance. Rather than resenting the way she twists his comments, he is amused by her cleverness. He realises the 'danger' of conversation with someone of her wit and intelligence. The word 'danger' has already been used in this context in Chapter X (Chapter 10), and the repetition of this strong word, placed in such a significant position in the last sentence of the chapter, marks a further point in the development of Darcy's interest.

In Volume Three, Chapter XVIII (Chapter 60) they discuss this phase in their relationship. Darcy admits he admired Elizabeth's 'liveliness of mind', which she calls 'impudence' (p. 306). And she puts forward the view that it was her refusal to try to please him (implicitly, in the manner of Caroline Bingley) that made her attractive. Austen recognises the peculiar ways in which attraction and love function.

VOLUME ONE, CHAPTER XII (CHAPTER 12)

SUMMARY

- Mrs Bennet refuses Elizabeth's request for a carriage to be sent: she wants Jane to spend as long as possible in the company of Bingley.
- The sisters ask to borrow the Bingley carriage. They are prevailed upon to stay another night by Bingley, who is sorry to see them go the following day.
- Darcy is pleased that Elizabeth is going and pointedly ignores her in case she guesses the effect that she has had on him.
- Jane and Elizabeth return to Longbourn.

ANALYSIS

RETURN TO LONGBOURN

Upon their arrival, Mrs Bennet is cross that they have not stayed longer but their father is pleased to have them back at home. Austen tells us: 'The evening conversation, when they were all assembled, had lost much of its animation, and almost all its sense, by the absence of Jane and Elizabeth' (p. 59). Mary is studying and is as pedantic as ever. We learn of Catherine and Lydia's latest discoveries regarding the officers and their movements. Although Mrs Bennet did not welcome her daughters 'very cordially' (p. 59), we sense that Jane and Elizabeth are relieved to be home. Certainly Elizabeth left Netherfield 'in the liveliest spirits' (p. 59).

STUDY FOCUS: AUSTEN'S NARRATION `A02`

Little of this short chapter is dramatised – unusually, there is no **dialogue**. It provides an interesting example of Austen's **omniscient narration**. Darcy's peculiar behaviour in relation to Elizabeth, refusing even to look at her, is not directly commented upon by the author (though the reader must wonder what to feel about it). However, the narrator's description of Mary and her 'thread-bare morality' (p. 59) is more clearly judgemental.

GRADE BOOSTER `A02`

Look closely at Miss Bingley's words and actions in the chapters set in Netherfield. How would you describe her behaviour? How can her sudden increase in 'civility' be explained?

CRITICAL VIEWPOINT `A04`

Carol Shields writes: 'It is difficult to love Darcy, though readers are attracted to something glittering and hard in his personality.' As you read on, consider how far you agree with this statement.

GLOSSARY

| 58 | **propitious** favourable |
| 59 | **thorough bass** harmony |

VOLUME ONE, CHAPTERS XIII AND XIV (CHAPTERS 13 AND 14)

SUMMARY

- Mr Bennet tells his family that his cousin, Mr Collins (who will eventually inherit Longbourn), is coming to dinner. Mr Bennet has never met Mr Collins because of a quarrel with his father.
- In his letter Mr Collins explains that he is a clergyman in the patronage of a Lady Catherine de Bourgh in Hunsford in Kent and proposes to visit the family for a week.
- Mr Collins is described as being punctual, formal and rather self-important.
- Led on by Mr Bennet, Mr Collins praises his patroness, Lady Catherine de Bourgh, and her kindness to him. She has advised him to get married.
- Mr Collins is invited to read to the company. He chooses a book of sermons. Lydia is soon bored and rudely interrupts him. Mr Collins is much offended and refuses to continue, preferring to play backgammon with Mr Bennet.

ANALYSIS

REACTIONS TO MR COLLINS'S LETTER

After the reading of Mr Collins's letter, the Bennets all react to its **style** and content. These comments and reactions are used to contrast their characters and perceptions. Mrs Bennet – who previously could not bear the thought of him or the entailment of the property – is immediately placated (not least because his heavy hints suggest he is thinking of marrying one of her girls). Jane approves of his good intentions, Elizabeth questions his sense and immediately declares him an 'oddity' (p. 62), Mary commends his unoriginal but precise way with words, and Catherine and Lydia are not interested as he is not a soldier. Mr Bennet, meanwhile, looks forward to the quiet enjoyment of Mr Collins's folly: 'There is a mixture of servility and self-importance in his letter, which promises well. I am impatient to see him' (p. 63). The reader may be feeling similarly impatient to meet Mr Collins.

STUDY FOCUS: HOW AUSTEN PRESENTS MR COLLINS · A02

This chapter is structured in such a way as to manoeuvre the reader into a clear understanding of what kind of person Mr Collins is. His letter reveals an astonishing pomposity, and his sentences are leaden and have too many clauses. In both its sentiments and its **style**, the letter reveals a degree of self-importance and snobbery that borders on **parody**. Later in the chapter, Collins arrives and compliments Mrs Bennet on the beauty of her daughters in dry and conventional terms. He is all admiration for Longbourn and its contents, though Austen reminds us that everything he sees is 'his future property' (p. 64). The way in which Mr Collins's conversation is initially related, rather than reproduced, and then the sheer length of his utterances when Austen does use **direct speech**, deny vitality to his character. The reader's reactions are also guided by Mr Bennet, who finds his cousin 'as absurd as he hoped' (p. 67).

GLOSSARY

65	**quadrille**	a card game
66	**phaeton**	a four-wheeled open carriage
67	**Fordyce's Sermons**	James Fordyce's *Sermons to Young Women* (1766)

CONTEXT · A04

The Bennets' home is tied up in an unbreakable legal arrangement where it can only be left to male heirs – and Mr Bennet has five daughters. In the event of his death the house will pass to the nearest male relative, Mr Collins, and the Bennet women will have nowhere to live. This fossil of a patriarchal legal system based on primogeniture (the right of a first-born son to inherit the entire estate) is criticised even by such a stickler for tradition as Lady Catherine de Bourgh in Volume Two, Book VI (Chapter 29).

GRADE BOOSTER · A02

Mr Collins's objection to reading a novel is not an untypical reaction for a serious clergyman in the early nineteenth century, though it may be contrasted with some of his other behaviour: is backgammon more worthwhile than reading fiction or dancing (see Chapter XVII (Chapter 17))? Of course, for such a character to make this point from within the pages of a novel is itself comic. Who reads, and what they read, is a matter for debate at several points in the novel – compare, for example, the discussion in Chapter VIII (Chapter 8).

VOLUME ONE, CHAPTER XV (CHAPTER 15)

SUMMARY

- Mr Collins plans to marry one of the Bennet daughters, thereby resolving the problem of the entailment. When Mrs Bennet warns him that Jane is 'likely to be very soon engaged' (p. 70), he decides to focus on Elizabeth.
- All of the sisters but Mary walk with Mr Collins to Meryton, where they meet a Mr Wickham. Darcy and Wickham recognise each other.
- Mr Collins is presented to Mrs Philips, the sister of Mrs Bennet. He is overly polite and verbose.
- A dinner is planned to which Wickham will be invited.

ANALYSIS

MR COLLINS'S CHARACTER

We learn more of Mr Collins's weak character and poor education 'under the guidance of an illiterate and miserly father' (p. 69) at the beginning of this chapter. Austen's description of Mr Collins in Mr Bennet's library further illustrates this deficiency. Whereas for Mr Bennet the library is a place of 'leisure and tranquility' (p. 70), Mr Collins's concentration and interest in the library's contents are somewhat lacking and he is 'extremely well pleased to close his large book, and go' (p. 70). The reader might be reminded of the difference between Bingley's and Darcy's libraries in Chapter VIII (Chapter 8) and what the reader infers about the two men as a consequence.

Mr Collins's mixture of 'pride and obsequiousness, self-importance and humility' (p. 69) is condemned outright by the **narrator**. His delight in his own plan to marry one of the Bennet daughters is further evidence of these characteristics: 'This was his plan … and he thought it an excellent one, full of eligibility and suitableness, and excessively generous and disinterested on his own part' (p. 69). His easy and swift transference of this interest from one daughter to another is almost shocking in its complacency, and requires no authorial comment. The detail that he undergoes this change of heart 'while Mrs Bennet was stirring the fire' (p. 70) is condemnation enough.

STUDY FOCUS: WICKHAM THE STRANGER A02

First impressions of Mr Wickham are that he is agreeable and handsome. Indeed 'all were struck with the stranger's air, all wondered who he could be' (p. 71). The discovery, on being introduced, that Mr Wickham is an officer makes him the image of a 'completely charming' (p. 71) gentleman in the younger sisters' eyes.

However, when Darcy and Bingley join the group, Darcy's strange reaction creates a mystery that it will take a large part of the novel to solve. We are told that 'Both changed colour, one looked white, the other red' and Darcy 'just deigned to return' Wickham's salutation (p. 72). Suspense is generated for Elizabeth and the reader: 'What could be the meaning of it?—It was impossible to imagine; it was impossible not to long to know' (p. 72). Elizabeth has noticed both men's discomfort and, like us, is eager to know the history of their acquaintance.

VOLUME ONE, CHAPTERS XVI AND XVII (CHAPTERS 16 AND 17)

SUMMARY

- The Longbourn party travels to Mrs Philips's house.

- Wickham explains that his father was steward of the Darcy estate and that Wickham was a favourite of Darcy's late father. He tells Elizabeth that Mr Darcy deprived him of a good living in the church. Elizabeth is outraged.

- Jane and Elizabeth discuss Wickham, Darcy and Bingley. Jane is reluctant to believe ill of Darcy and attributes his behaviour to some misunderstanding.

- The Netherfield ball is anticipated with delight, though Elizabeth's excitement is tempered by the increasing attention Mr Collins is giving her.

ANALYSIS

LADY CATHERINE DE BOURGH

We learn that Catherine de Bourgh, Mr Collins's much esteemed patron, is Darcy's aunt and that Darcy is destined to marry her daughter. To confirm Elizabeth's impression of Lady Catherine's conceitedness, Wickham criticises her 'dictatorial and insolent' manners though he concedes that she has a reputation for being 'remarkably sensible and clever' (p. 82). Elizabeth smiles when she discovers that Darcy and Lady Catherine's daughter are widely expected to marry, since she sees that Caroline Bingley's pursuit of Darcy for herself will be in vain. While we have not directly encountered Lady Catherine de Bourgh as yet, we may gather that she is an influential and formidable character.

ELIZABETH AND COLLINS

Like all her sisters, Elizabeth looks forward to the ball at Netherfield and especially to dancing with Wickham. However, Mr Collins asks Elizabeth to dance the first two dances with him, an offer Elizabeth is compelled to accept albeit reluctantly. We are told that 'Elizabeth felt herself completely taken in' and that 'her liveliness had never been worse timed!' (p. 86) since it was she who approached Mr Collins to ask whether he intended to attend the ball and to dance. She realises now that she is the object of his marital intentions, and that while she feels 'more astonished than gratified' by this realisation, the prospect is of course 'exceedingly agreeable' to her mother (p. 87).

STUDY FOCUS: WICKHAM AND DARCY A02

Chapter XVI (Chapter 16) consists almost entirely of the conversation between Elizabeth and Wickham focusing on Darcy's pride. Given what happens later in the novel, this encounter must be examined in detail. Should Elizabeth have recognised something in Wickham's manner that might have betrayed his true nature? Does her prejudice against Darcy blind her to the inappropriate frankness of Wickham's conversation? How much is she swayed by Wickham's pleasing appearance?

In Chapter XVII (Chapter 17), Elizabeth and Jane differ in their view of Wickham. Jane always tries to see the best in everyone; Elizabeth has a less charitable view, and is perfectly certain in her condemnation of Darcy: 'one knows exactly what to think' (p. 85). So far our sympathies are all with Elizabeth, who seems to have the same kind of intelligent (if **ironic**) grasp of events as her father and the narrator.

VOLUME ONE, CHAPTER XVIII (CHAPTER 18)

SUMMARY

- Mr Wickham is not at the ball and, to make matters worse for Elizabeth, dancing with Mr Collins proves to be a mortifying experience.
- Elizabeth is talking to Charlotte Lucas when they are surprised by Darcy and, almost by mistake, Elizabeth accepts his request for a dance. Conversation is awkward, but 'unable to resist the temptation' (p. 90) Elizabeth refers to Wickham.
- Jane believes that Bingley admires her and she is very happy. Meanwhile, Mr Collins pays Elizabeth much attention although Charlotte Lucas often joins them and talks to Mr Collins herself, for which diversion Elizabeth is grateful.

ANALYSIS

CONFLICTING VIEWS OF WICKHAM

Darcy is troubled by Elizabeth's interest in Wickham and changes the subject after remarking that Wickham makes friends easily but that 'whether he may be equally capable of retaining them, is less certain' (p. 91). Elizabeth considers that Darcy is exhibiting prejudice towards Wickham. In retrospect, we see that it is she who is prejudiced. Miss Bingley tells Elizabeth that Wickham has treated Darcy in a most 'infamous manner' (p. 80) and makes pointed remarks about Elizabeth's supposed interest in him. Jane reports more criticism of Wickham, this time from Bingley, but Elizabeth distrusts this opinion as coming from Darcy.

STUDY FOCUS: SOCIAL COMEDY — A02

After supper (at which Mrs Bennet has once again chattered away indiscreetly), Mary sings for too long (only stopping after remonstrations from her father) and Mr Collins makes a loud and superfluous speech on music and the duties of the clergy. Mrs Bennet, Mary and Mr Collins are the butts of Austen's **social comedy**, but here it is laced with the pain of Elizabeth's embarrassment. It is difficult to know how to react to these complex circumstances, so typical of Austen, who refuses to sentimentalise family life: our heroine's mother is stupid and offensive; three of her sisters are boring or silly; her cousin is a monster of conceited self-importance. Can the reader take pleasure in the garishness of the occasion as Mr Bennet does? Do we thereby share some of Miss Bingley's snobbery and contempt, and Darcy's 'hauteur'? How does the comedy conflict with our sympathies for Elizabeth?

CRITICAL VIEWPOINT A03

The novelist Charlotte Brontë criticised *Pride and Prejudice* for offering 'no glance of a bright, vivid physiognomy, no open country, no fresh air ... I should hardly like to live with her ladies and gentlemen, in their elegant but confined homes.'

CHECK THE FILM A03

The BBC version of these scenes, in which several members of the Bennet family disgrace themselves, is particularly and accurately painful. Memories of this ball infuse the letter Darcy writes to Elizabeth after his failed proposal, which she ponders in Volume Two, Chapters XII and XIII (Chapters 35 and 36).

GLOSSARY

99 **tythes** – a clergyman was entitled to a tenth of the income from all cultivated land within his parish (also spelt 'tithes')

VOLUME ONE, CHAPTERS XIX AND XX (CHAPTERS 19 AND 20)

SUMMARY

- Mr Collins proposes to Elizabeth, describing it as his religious duty and a means to smooth over his inheritance of Longbourn. She refuses him repeatedly. Mr Collins, however, believes her refusals to be 'merely words of course' (p. 106).
- Her father forbids her to accept the proposal whereas Mrs Bennet berates her wayward daughter for being a 'very headstrong foolish girl' who 'does not know her own interest' (p. 108).
- Mr Collins eventually withdraws his proposal.

ANALYSIS

REACTIONS TO THE PROPOSAL

The dilemma in which her father places Elizabeth – that she will lose the affection of her mother if she refuses Mr Collins, but his affection if she accepts – is not really a dilemma at all. Mr Bennet knows his wife and daughter well enough to be certain of the outcome. Austen provides a variety of perspectives on the farcical confusion, without any direct comment. For Lydia, it is 'such fun' (p. 110), Jane 'with all possible mildness declined interfering' (p. 110), and Mrs Bennet is locked in her absurd self-pity: 'Nobody can tell what I suffer!' (p. 111).

Mr Bennet dominates the domestic melodrama with his usual **ironic** detachment. We may wonder if his attitude borders on the facetious: though he supports Elizabeth's (and the reader's) view of Mr Collins, he seems interested chiefly in concluding the situation with a witticism and getting everyone out of his study. Meanwhile, Charlotte Lucas is a quiet but curious observer of the events of Chapter XX (Chapter 20).

STUDY FOCUS: MR COLLINS'S LANGUAGE OF LOVE

Mr Collins's speech is stilted, pompous and governed by egotism. His pedantic style leads him to break down his speech into numbered points – 'first … Secondly … thirdly' (p. 103) – which are unsuitable in a proposal of marriage. Elizabeth nearly laughs at the idea of Mr Collins 'being run away with by his feelings' (p. 103), given the incongruity of such a description with his careful and passionless manner. He goes on to show that he has not considered her views or feelings, so certain is he of the generosity of his offer: 'My situation in life, my connections with the family of De Bourgh, and my relationship to your own, are circumstances highly in my favour' (p. 106). Indeed, the feelings and opinions of Lady Catherine appear to occupy Mr Collins's thoughts far more than those of Lizzy.

The scene is richly comic, but harsh realities underlie the situation. Mr Collins reminds Elizabeth that since she has so little money to her name, she may never receive another offer of marriage 'in spite of your manifold attractions' (p. 106). The economic realities of wedlock appear in their most unattractive and unromantic light here. The following chapter concludes with Mr Collins's withdrawal: once again, it is long-winded, pedantic and self-centred – a **parody** of male egocentricity.

VOLUME ONE, CHAPTER XXI (CHAPTER 21)

SUMMARY

- Following his unsuccessful proposal, Mr Collins is silent and resentful towards Elizabeth. He spends time talking to Charlotte Lucas, for which Elizabeth is grateful. Mrs Bennet is still angry with her daughter.

- The girls walk to Meryton and meet Wickham. He confesses to Elizabeth that he stayed away from the ball to avoid being in the same room as Darcy. Elizabeth is pleased by his attentions.

- Jane and Elizabeth learn in a letter from Caroline Bingley that the Bingleys have left Netherfield for the winter. The sisters discuss this news.

ANALYSIS

THE BINGLEYS LEAVE NETHERFIELD

Jane is clearly upset by the contents of Caroline Bingley's letter. When she and Elizabeth are alone, Jane reads extracts and explains the letter's substance to Elizabeth. Miss Bingley describes Georgiana Darcy – 'I really do not think Georgiana Darcy has her equal for beauty, elegance and accomplishments' (p. 116) – and mentions her hope that Bingley will marry her. Jane is discouraged and believes that Miss Bingley is trying to let her know that Bingley is not interested in her. Elizabeth's interpretation differs entirely. She thinks that Bingley has been whisked away because his sisters do not want him to marry Jane but that his feelings for Jane remain constant: 'you cannot seriously imagine that … he is in the smallest degree less sensible of your merit than when he took leave of you on Tuesday' (p. 117).

STUDY FOCUS: OPPOSING INTERPRETATIONS

In their opposed readings of the letter, Elizabeth and Jane present a model that suggests how we as readers should examine the events of the novel: every detail is scrutinised in order to infer meaning and motive, yet the text itself remains ambiguous and inscrutable. There is nothing that can lend certainty to either mutually exclusive view; all is possible, and only future events will show which sister, if either, was right in her surmise. Elizabeth's view is the more optimistic about the constancy of Bingley's feelings, even though she sees the letter as an ill-intentioned sisterly ploy, while Jane sees things at their worst in the long term, viewing the letter as a friendly warning.

KEY QUOTATION: VOLUME ONE, CHAPTER XXI (CHAPTER 21)

Key quotation: 'He scarcely ever spoke to her, and the assiduous attentions … were transferred for the rest of the day to Miss Lucas, whose civility in listening to him, was a seasonable relief to them all, and especially to her friend.' (p. 113)

- This is one of a series of authorial hints to the reader, not only that Mr Collins is pleased to converse with Charlotte but also that she does not remotely resist his attentions.

- Austen's phrase 'civility in listening to him' suggests that Charlotte too finds him long-winded and that her feelings towards him are polite but far from passionate.

- The phrase 'especially to her friend' gives the reader the impression that Elizabeth is all too happy with this arrangement; we may conclude that she does not guess that her friend might be open to Mr Collins's advances.

CRITICAL VIEWPOINT A02

Carol Shields has written of the pace and structure of Austen's novels: 'She mastered, early on, the ability to move scenes briskly along. Moments of perceived interaction contrast sharply with abrupt psychological shifts. Always there is the sense that she knows where she's going, even in the midst of a digression. This assured narrative voice anchors and sustains the human drama, and it is a particular pleasure for the reader to find important moments buried in paragraphs that pretend to be flattened asides.'

CHECK THE BOOK A03

How does Mr Collins react to his rejection by Elizabeth? Compare this with Jane's concerns about the continuation of Bingley's affections for her. Look at how the theme of rejection in love and marriage is treated in other novels such as John Fowles's *The French Lieutenant's Woman* (1969) and Charlotte Brontë's *Jane Eyre* (1847).

GLOSSARY

114 **hot pressed paper** fine, expensive writing paper

114 **Grosvenor street** a fashionable residential area of London

VOLUME ONE, CHAPTERS XXII AND XXIII (CHAPTERS 22 AND 23)

SUMMARY

- Mr Collins proposes to Charlotte and is accepted. She breaks the news to Elizabeth.
- Sir William Lucas visits in order to announce his daughter's engagement. Mrs Bennet and Lydia initially refuse to believe him.
- Bingley stays in London and Elizabeth worries that his sisters will be successful in preventing him from seeing Jane.

ANALYSIS

MR COLLINS'S PROPOSAL TO CHARLOTTE

Austen's description of Mr Collins's proposal to Charlotte is highly **ironic**, even acidic, almost expressing hatred. (For further discussion of this, see the section on **Irony** in **Part Four: Language**.) This chapter reveals the chilling version of marriage that is so very different to a union based on true 'affection' (p. 22). Mr Collins's method of courtship is described as so charmless that 'no woman could wish for its continuance' (p. 120) and we are told directly that Charlotte accepts her suitor's proposal 'solely from the pure and disinterested desire of an establishment' (p. 120).

Charlotte has appraised her own situation and decides that marriage is 'the only honourable provision for well-educated young women of small fortune, and however uncertain of giving happiness, must be their pleasantest preservative from want' (p. 120). For their part, the Lucas family are delighted, and start to speculate about Mr Bennet's death, when their daughter will take possession of Longbourn.

THE BENNETS

By contrast, things are going badly for the Bennet family, especially Mrs Bennet, whose marriage plans for her daughters are falling apart. Her distress and incredulity are summed up in her muddled tirade after Sir William leaves Longbourn: 'her feelings found a rapid vent' (p. 125). She cannot bear to hear anything concerning Charlotte Lucas and cannot forgive her daughter Lizzy's part in the whole sorry business. Mr Bennet takes refuge in the philosophical reflection that 'Charlotte Lucas, whom he had been used to think tolerably sensible, was as foolish as his wife, and more foolish than his daughter!' (p. 125).

To add to their woes, Mr Collins reappears at Longbourn and furthermore Jane's 'early answer' to Caroline Bingley's letter has not met with a reply. Jane's anxiety is compounded by her mother's frequent comments on the subject, and Austen remarks that 'It needed all Jane's steady mildness to bear these attacks with tolerable tranquillity' (p. 127).

STUDY FOCUS: LIZZY'S AND CHARLOTTE'S CONTRASTING VIEWS

Elizabeth is astonished at her friend's mercenary decision. Her first reaction on hearing the news that Charlotte has accepted Collins's proposal is that it is 'impossible' (p. 122). She cannot imagine that Charlotte will ever be 'tolerably happy' (p. 123). The reader, thanks to authorial hints and irony, has expected Mr Collins to propose to Charlotte, and knows Charlotte's cynical views. Yet Elizabeth, for all her astuteness of observation, has entirely mistaken her best friend's nature.

GRADE BOOSTER A02

In Chapter XXIII (Chapter 23), we hear that the friendship between Charlotte and Elizabeth is under strain. Elizabeth fears that 'no real confidence could ever subsist between them again' (p. 125). Examine the theme of friendship as it develops throughout *Pride and Prejudice*.

GLOSSARY

120 **coming out** a young woman's entry into society

125 **rectitude** morally correct behaviour or thinking

VOLUME TWO, CHAPTERS I AND II (CHAPTERS 24 AND 25)

SUMMARY

- The much-awaited letter from Miss Bingley arrives. The Bingleys will definitely not return to Netherfield all winter and it is implied that Bingley and Miss Darcy will marry.
- Mr Wickham is often in the Longbourn household. He has told many people of his suffering at the hands of Darcy. Jane is the only one ever to defend Darcy.
- Mr Collins returns to Hunsford, planning an early wedding. Mrs Bennet's brother Mr Gardiner and his wife visit for Christmas and Jane returns to London with them.

ANALYSIS

JANE AND ELIZABETH

On receiving the letter from Miss Bingley, Jane is determined to forget her attachment to Bingley, since she is sure that she was mistaken in imagining that he admired her: 'it has not been more than an error of fancy on my side' (p. 132). Elizabeth believes that he likes Jane as much as ever, but that he has yielded to the wills of his sisters and Darcy. Previously the opinions of Elizabeth have been supported by Austen's depiction of events. Here, Jane's rational reaction to Charlotte's marriage may appear to be more justified than Elizabeth's incredulity. We find that Elizabeth has begun to feel dissatisfied and let down by 'the inconsistency of all human characters, and … the little dependence that can be placed on the appearance of either merit or sense' (p. 133), whereas Jane calmly advises her sister to allow 'for difference of situation and temper' (p. 133) when reflecting on the behaviour of others.

STUDY FOCUS: THE GARDINERS | A02

When the Gardiners arrive at Longbourn in Chapter II (Chapter 25), we are told that Mr Gardiner is 'a sensible, gentlemanlike man, greatly superior to his sister as well by nature as by education' (p. 137). Mrs Gardiner – 'an amiable, intelligent, elegant woman' – is a 'great favourite with all her Longbourn nieces' (p. 137) and a particular friend to the two eldest Bennet girls. Mrs Gardiner talks to Elizabeth about Jane and Bingley, and 'narrowly observe[s]' (p. 140) Elizabeth with Wickham. Mrs Gardiner was originally from Derbyshire and is familiar with Pemberley, Darcy's estate. She enjoys discussing Pemberley and the late Mr Darcy with Wickham.

Austen draws a contrast between Mrs Gardiner's good sense and sensitivity and Mrs Bennet's vapid nature. We see Mrs Bennet's mind easily switch from discussing the serious events of her daughter's aborted engagements to gossip about the latest fashions: 'I am very glad to hear what you tell us, of long sleeves' (p. 138). Mrs Gardiner is a very different character and perhaps represents the kind of mother that Elizabeth should have had. She takes over as Elizabeth's interlocutor (the person with whom she is in conversation) and gives a fresh new perspective on events – 'these sort of inconstancies are very frequent' (p. 138) and 'It had better have happened to you, Lizzy; you would have laughed yourself out of it sooner' (p. 139). She is also practical, suggesting that Jane return to London with them for a 'change of scene' (p. 139).

GRADE BOOSTER | A02

Mr Bennet's ironies – 'Let Wickham be *your* man. He is a pleasant fellow, and would jilt you creditably' (p. 135) – may suggest that he knows something about Wickham of which Elizabeth is ignorant. Is he by his comment warning Elizabeth, whose partiality for Wickham he has noticed, or is he just enjoying the free play of his irony?

CONTEXT | A03

In the original format of the novel, the first volume finished with Chapter 23 and the second volume began with Chapter 24.

GLOSSARY

132 and 139 **solicitude** care or concern for something or someone

139 **Gracechurch Street** in the City of London, about two miles away from where the Hursts live

VOLUME TWO, CHAPTER III (CHAPTER 26)

SUMMARY

- Mrs Gardiner reminds Elizabeth how ill-advised a match with Wickham would be.
- On the day before her wedding, Charlotte asks Elizabeth to visit her in Hunsford and, after the wedding, they become correspondents.
- Jane has been snubbed by the Bingleys in London and it appears that Bingley intends to stop leasing Netherfield. Jane acknowledges that Elizabeth was correct in her judgement of Bingley's sisters.
- Wickham courts an heiress, Miss King.

ANALYSIS

ELIZABETH AND WICKHAM

Mrs Gardiner, having observed Elizabeth's preferential treatment of Wickham, tries to dissuade her from the relationship. She reminds Elizabeth that Wickham is not suitable for her financially or socially. Elizabeth promises to do her best, although she does not promise not to fall in love with him: 'how can I promise to be wiser than so many of my fellow creatures?' (p. 143).

At the end of the chapter, Elizabeth writes to her aunt to tell her that Wickham's attentions have ceased. He is now the admirer of a certain Miss King, who has recently inherited ten thousand pounds. We are shown that Elizabeth is able to smile at Wickham's courting someone richer than herself by the pun on the word 'fortune', meaning both luck and financial advantage: '*she* would have been his only choice, had fortune permitted it' (p. 147).

STUDY FOCUS: LETTER-WRITING **A02**

Following the wedding, we read that Charlotte and Elizabeth's correspondence is 'as regular and frequent as it had ever been' though Elizabeth still feels that 'all the comfort of intimacy was over' (p. 144). Charlotte writes of her new home and husband with reserve and discretion 'and Elizabeth perceived that she must wait for her own visit there, to know the rest' (p. 144). Austen is focusing our attention far more on Elizabeth's reactions to the letters than on the letters themselves.

We also learn via Jane's letters to Elizabeth that Caroline Bingley has not visited her, and that when Jane called on Miss Bingley the visit was short and she saw neither Mr Bingley nor Miss Darcy. A month later Miss Bingley returns the visit, but her behaviour to Jane is much altered and even mild-mannered Jane is 'almost tempted to say, that there is a strong appearance of duplicity in all this' (p. 145). Austen includes this letter of Jane's in its entirety to 'prove what she felt' (p. 145).

Elizabeth's letter to Mrs Gardiner to relate that Wickham's 'apparent partiality had subsided' (p. 147) demonstrates Elizabeth's intelligence, resilience and perhaps even cynicism. Austen uses **free indirect speech** to follow Elizabeth's thought patterns, and then reports the latter part of the letter directly. The chapter ends with words that may recall the novel's aphoristic opening line: 'handsome young men must have something to live on, as well as the plain' (p. 148).

EXTENDED COMMENTARY

VOLUME TWO, CHAPTER III (CHAPTER 26), P. 144

This is not a crucial or dramatic passage, but rather a piece of **narratorial** summary linking scenes and events. Information is provided about Elizabeth's view of Charlotte over a passage of time. It is a source of sadness to Elizabeth that she no longer feels friendship for Charlotte. She will still honour her promise to visit, and correspond, though this will be a matter of duty rather than of pleasure. Marriage is not depicted as always spelling the end of friendship between women, but marriage to Mr Collins is such a disastrous step in Elizabeth's view that she cannot fully respect Charlotte's decision to pursue and accept him.

The passage is all about letters, and there are more letters in the rest of the chapter. It is easy to see traces of the lost original draft of *Pride and Prejudice*, which was possibly epistolary in form. Austen often uses reference to letters when she wants to advance the action through time quite quickly.

The description of Charlotte's wedding is squeezed into a sentence: 'The wedding took place, the bride and bridegroom set off for Kent from the church door, and every body had as much to say or to hear on the subject as usual' (p. 144). There is a distinction implied between those who have lots to say and those (less fortunate perhaps) who have to listen to them. Another pleasant opposition is between the loquacious wedding guests and the narrator's short way of describing the wedding.

In this case, 'every body' reminds us that in the background of the novel is constant talk, the 'news' that is Mrs Bennet's solace. Public opinion in the form of gossip is always something to contend with, a good example of which we can find later in the book in Volume Three, Chapter XIII (Chapter 55): 'the Bennets were speedily pronounced to be the luckiest family in the world, though only a few weeks before, when Lydia had first run away, they had generally proved to be marked out for misfortune' (p. 331).

Here Charlotte's letters are shown to be part of Elizabeth's inner life; they inform her way of thinking about her friend, but they are curiously disappointing, though they deal with life in Hunsford in exactly the cheerful, 'rationally softened' way that Elizabeth would have expected from Charlotte. Only the visit to Hunsford will allow her to 'know the rest'. Does she want Charlotte to admit her mistake in marrying Mr Collins?

Movement from the public to the private, from a dramatised scene to Elizabeth's thought processes, as in this passage, is a constant element in *Pride and Prejudice*. Elizabeth's reading of the letters allows a view of her consciousness that is different in effect, and less immediate, than the **free indirect style** used by Austen to reveal a character's thinking, often at moments of stress. Here we are shown a developing meditation on a topic over a period of time.

VOLUME TWO, CHAPTER IV (CHAPTER 27)

SUMMARY

- Wickham and Elizabeth part extremely amicably.
- Elizabeth travels with Sir William Lucas and his daughter Maria to stay with Charlotte Collins, visiting Jane on the way.
- In London Mrs Gardiner tells Elizabeth that Jane has been quite unhappy. Elizabeth agrees to a future trip to the Lake District with her aunt and uncle.

ANALYSIS

LIFE AT LONGBOURN

January and February are described as passing by with little in the way of incident or diversion other than 'the walks to Meryton, sometimes dirty and sometimes cold' (p. 149). In a tone that is perhaps symptomatic of this dreariness, Mr Bennet, roused by his pain at Elizabeth's going away, asks her to write to him 'and almost promised to answer her letter' (p. 149). Even a visit to Mr and Mrs Collins begins to seem attractive – 'Absence had increased her desire of seeing Charlotte again, and weakened her disgust of Mr Collins' (p. 149) – and Elizabeth looks forward to her visit to Hunsford in March. After all, 'with such a mother and such uncompanionable sisters, home could not be faultless' (p. 149).

STUDY FOCUS: MATRIMONIAL AFFAIRS   A02

Elizabeth discusses Wickham's new attachment to Miss King with Mrs Gardiner, and she speaks **ironically** of men and love. Her aunt warns her against sounding so bitter. However, Elizabeth enjoys teasing her aunt about Wickham: 'what is the difference in matrimonial affairs, between the mercenary and the prudent motive? Where does discretion end, and avarice begin?' (p. 151). Elizabeth astutely points out that Mrs Gardiner's earlier advice to her had been more about financial prudence than love or compatibility, and does not believe that the speed of Wickham's attachment to Miss King is indelicate or objectionable as her aunt does.

This discussion forms part of the debate that runs throughout the book about the role of money in romance and marriage. Elizabeth claims to be heartily sick of the whole business, and the mooted Lake District trip proves a welcome antidote: 'What are men to rocks and mountains?' (p. 152).

KEY QUOTATION: VOLUME TWO, CHAPTER IV (CHAPTER 27)   A01

Key quotation: 'Sir William Lucas, and his daughter Maria, a good humoured girl, but as empty-headed as himself, had nothing to say that could be worth hearing, and were listened to with about as much delight as the rattle of the chaise' (p. 150).

- Austen's characteristic sharp wit and comic skills are much in evidence in this short passage describing Elizabeth's fellow travellers.
- While we can be sure that Elizabeth conducted herself politely throughout her journey, the reader gains access to her less tolerant inner thoughts.
- There is great economy in the way that Austen conveys these impressions. In particular, she draws unfavourable comparisons to show the extent of Elizabeth's boredom.

CONTEXT   A03

The aesthetic appreciation of picturesque scenery was common from the mid-eighteenth century onwards. The landscape of the Lake District is a central preoccupation of the poetry of William Wordsworth (1770–1850), who himself wrote 'A Description of the Scenery of the Lakes in the North of England' as an introduction to T. Wilkinson's *Select Views in Cumberland* (1812).

GRADE BOOSTER   A02

To what extent do you think Austen might be **satirising** the Romantic era's love of the natural world with Elizabeth's outburst at the end of this chapter?

GLOSSARY

152   **transport** here used in the sense of great excitement

VOLUME TWO, CHAPTER V (CHAPTER 28)

SUMMARY

- Elizabeth, Sir William and Maria arrive at the Parsonage. Charlotte is pleased to see her friend, and Mr Collins is as formal and pompous as ever.
- Mr Collins shows them his house and grounds and prepares the guests for the honour of meeting Lady Catherine.
- News of Hertfordshire is exchanged. Miss De Bourgh passes by the Parsonage in her carriage and invites everyone to dine at Rosings the following evening.
- Elizabeth and Maria catch sight of Miss De Bourgh, declaring her 'quite a little creature' (p. 156).

ANALYSIS

ELIZABETH'S OPINIONS

Most of this chapter is concerned with reviving the comic description of Mr Collins through his pride in his 'humble abode' (p. 130), his garden and his noble neighbour. Sir William and Maria Lucas make good foils for his artless self-importance. The reader is privy to Elizabeth's curiosity as to how her friend Charlotte copes with such a husband, and we see that she is rather impressed by her arrangements: 'every thing was fitted up and arranged with a neatness and consistency of which Elizabeth gave Charlotte all the credit' (p. 155). Later in the chapter, Elizabeth takes cruel pleasure in finding Miss De Bourgh 'sickly and cross' (p. 156), and therefore a fitting wife for Darcy.

STUDY FOCUS: FORESHADOWING **A02**

Darcy has been very much in the background of the novel for the past few chapters, but Austen often shows Elizabeth's thoughts turning strangely swiftly to him as they do here when she first sees Miss De Bourgh. Is her ongoing negativity towards Darcy akin to attraction? In Volume One, Chapter XVI (Chapter 16), Elizabeth, on hearing that Darcy is destined to marry Miss De Bourgh, thinks of Miss Bingley's thwarted hopes (see also Volume Two, Chapters VII and VIII (Chapters 30 and 31)). Indeed, Darcy's future wife often springs to mind, though any thought of herself in this role is denied. In Volume One, Chapter VIII (Chapter 8), she is fascinated by the description of Pemberley, and puts down her book in order to be able to listen. All these are hints that **foreshadow** future events.

GRADE BOOSTER **A02**

How are the different houses in the novel (Longbourn, Netherfield, Pemberley, Hunsford Parsonage, Rosings, etc.) described and what do these descriptions show us or suggest to us about the characters who inhabit them?

CHECK THE FILM **A04**

How does the BBC version show us Elizabeth's inner thought processes? Try watching the way it presents Elizabeth reading Darcy's letter in Chapter XII (Chapter 35).

VOLUME TWO, CHAPTER VI (CHAPTER 29)

SUMMARY

- Lady Catherine and her guests dine at Rosings. Sir William and Maria are overawed but Elizabeth feels equal to the experience. Lady Catherine is arrogant, self-important, overbearing and opinionated.

- Lady Catherine quizzes Elizabeth about her family and origins and is shocked to hear that the five Bennet girls were brought up without a governess. She asks how many of Elizabeth's sisters are 'out' and demands to know her age.

ANALYSIS

MR COLLINS AND HIS PATRON

Mr Collins is overjoyed to be able to display 'the grandeur of his patroness' (p. 157) to his visitors so soon during their visit. When he talked about her in Chapter V (Chapter 28), he spoke to his guests of 'the honour of seeing her' and explained that 'she is the sort of woman whom one cannot regard with too much deference' (p. 155). His excited behaviour in Chapter VI (Chapter 29) follows suit as talk of the

visit dominates the whole day and the next morning. He prepares his guests in minute detail for the grandeur of Rosings, and reassures Elizabeth that her best clothes will be sufficient to preserve differences in rank.

STUDY FOCUS: LADY CATHERINE DE BOURGH `A02`

Lady Catherine de Bourgh is one of the great comic creations of the novel. She is an appalling snob, utterly complacent in her sense of her own exalted status – 'Her air was not conciliating, nor was her manner of receiving them, such as to make her visitors forget their inferior rank' (p. 159) – and convinced of the absolute rightness of all her opinions on all subjects. We are told that she speaks 'on every subject in so decisive a manner as proved that she was not used to have her judgement controverted' (p. 160).

When the women find themselves alone, she inquires into every aspect of Charlotte's housekeeping. Lady Catherine is also extremely rude in presuming to comment so freely on Elizabeth's upbringing. However, the novel's events suggest that there may be some truth in her views; certainly we know that Elizabeth herself feels her young sisters are lacking in either self-discipline or parental control. Lady Catherine also has views on the entail with which Mrs Bennet would sympathise: her family estate was not entailed from the female line, and so she and her daughter are financially independent. Despite this, it is left to Elizabeth and the **narrator** to see Lady Catherine for what she is, though of course Elizabeth answers her impertinent questions 'very composedly' (p. 160).

GRADE BOOSTER `A02`

Compare Austen's presentation of Lady Catherine de Bourgh in this chapter with the different descriptions of her we have previously heard from Mr Collins (Volume One, Chapter XIV (Chapter 14)) and Wickham (Volume One, Chapter XVI (Chapter 16)).

CHECK THE FILM `A04`

The monstrosity of Lady Catherine de Bourgh's dictatorial self-importance is very apparent in the BBC version, where her guests are shown sitting in lines attendant on her every word.

GLOSSARY

157 **toilette** dressing and grooming before going out

159 **placing a screen in the proper direction** to shield her from the direct heat of the fire

VOLUME TWO, CHAPTERS VII AND VIII (CHAPTERS 30 AND 31)

SUMMARY

- Sir William stays for a week and is convinced of Charlotte's good fortune in husband and neighbours.
- Mr Collins goes to call on the recently arrived Darcy and Colonel Fitzwilliam (another of Lady Catherine's nephews) and is accompanied back to the parsonage by the two men.
- Elizabeth tells Darcy that Jane has been in London and asks him if he has seen her. He seems embarrassed and replies in the negative.
- A week after the arrival of Darcy and Colonel Fitzwilliam, the parsonage party are invited to Rosings after church.

ANALYSIS

AT HUNSFORD PARSONAGE

Following Sir William's departure, another fortnight passes during which Elizabeth notes that Charlotte has wisely arranged the rooms of the house so as not to be perpetually in the company of her husband. Most days involve a visit to Rosings, and occasionally Lady Catherine returns the courtesy. They dine twice a week at Rosings. Elizabeth is pleased to be with Charlotte and is often outdoors, discovering a 'favourite walk … where she frequently went while the others were calling on Lady Catherine' (p. 165), further evidence of her independent nature.

A MUSICAL INTERLUDE

Lady Catherine claims to be a musical expert, though she cannot play herself, and repeatedly stresses her daughter's musical aptitude 'had her health allowed her to learn' (p. 172). Colonel Fitzwilliam persuades Elizabeth to play the piano forte. While Lady Catherine talks during her performance, Darcy seems to take an unusual interest in Elizabeth's playing and her face. Elizabeth and Darcy then have a teasing conversation in which Elizabeth reminds Darcy of not having asked her to dance in Hertfordshire. Elizabeth and Darcy assess each other's characters using the **extended metaphor** of practising and playing at the piano. 'We neither of us perform to strangers' (p. 171), concludes Darcy before Lady Catherine interrupts once again.

STUDY FOCUS: DARCY AND ELIZABETH   A02

This chapter advances the teasing, conversational sparring between Darcy and Elizabeth, at which she is an expert. Darcy comments rather woodenly on her ironic powers; he is by contrast inadequate and defensive, but not apparently unhappy to be the butt of her wit. His pride is dissolving. Elizabeth even seems to wonder at the nature of his attentions but could not 'discern any symptom of love' (p. 172). She appears genuinely puzzled by Darcy's attention to herself, but pleased to note no special feeling between him and his cousin Miss De Bourgh.

Most readers will have guessed by now that the novel's central relationship is between the two of them, and will be wondering how pride and prejudice will be overcome, or not.

CHECK THE FILM   A04

In discussions between Elizabeth and Charlotte about the arrangements at the parsonage, the BBC adaptation has to make explicit what is silently noted by Elizabeth in the text.

CONTEXT   A04

The piano forte (in which strings are struck rather than plucked, allowing it to be played both *piano* and *forte* – soft and loud) only became a common musical instrument in the last quarter of the eighteenth century. Lady Catherine, always keen to display her riches, has two, one of which is tucked away in the servants' quarters. Darcy's gift of a special piano for his sister is noted in Volume Three, Chapter I (Chapter 43), during the visit to Pemberley.

VOLUME TWO, CHAPTERS IX AND X (CHAPTERS 32 AND 33)

SUMMARY

- Darcy pays Elizabeth a solo visit. He confirms Jane's news that Bingley does not intend to spend much time at Netherfield in the future. Puzzlingly, Darcy remarks that she cannot have lived all her life at Longbourn. He often comes to the parsonage; Charlotte wonders why.

- Elizabeth keeps on meeting Darcy while she is walking. On another occasion, she is distressed by his implication that during some future visit she will stay at Rosings. Elizabeth thinks that he must be referring to a possible match between herself and Colonel Fitzwilliam.

- Colonel Fitzwilliam tells her that Darcy keeps delaying their departure and embarrasses Elizabeth somewhat by saying that 'there are not many in my rank of life who can afford to marry without some attention to money' (p. 179).

- Fitzwilliam also reveals that that he is a joint guardian of Georgiana with Darcy and that Darcy has prevented a friend from an ill-advised marriage to a woman against whom there were 'very strong objections' (p. 181). Elizabeth can only think of Bingley and Jane.

ANALYSIS

CHARLOTTE'S VIEW

Further visits from Darcy and Colonel Fitzwilliam lead Elizabeth to compare the latter to her former admirer Wickham, and Charlotte to wonder whether the former can be in love with Elizabeth: 'he must be in love with you, or he would never have called on us in this familiar way' (p. 175). Darcy is mostly silent on these visits but looks at her a great deal, though whether with love and admiration, or merely absentmindedness, is not clear. Charlotte 'knew not what to make of him' (p. 176) but is sure that Elizabeth would accept Darcy could she 'suppose him to be in her power' (p. 176). Comparing Fitzwilliam and Darcy as future husbands for her friend, she has the practical thought that, despite the fact that Fitzwilliam 'was beyond comparison the pleasantest man' (p. 177), Darcy is the one with 'considerable patronage in the church' (p. 177).

Charlotte's reflections on how quickly Elizabeth might fall for Darcy, and on the relative merits of Fitzwilliam and Darcy as prospective husbands for her friend, add to the novel's pragmatic consideration of marriage in terms of power and money. This may be perceived, in Charlotte and in the **narrator**, as either engagingly honest or distastefully unromantic.

INTERPRETATIONS AND MISINTERPRETATIONS

The reader needs to study Darcy's strange comments in this chapter, to evaluate what may be going on is his mind. When he says '*You* cannot have been always at Longbourn' (p. 175), is he clumsily suggesting that Elizabeth's sophistication could not have been acquired in her home? This is not much of a compliment as it reveals his prejudice against her family.

> **CHECK THE BOOK** **A04**
>
> Unlike Miss De Bourgh, Elizabeth Bennet is usually depicted as in the bloom of good health. For an examination of Austen's attitudes to illness, see J. Wiltshire's *Jane Austen and the Body* (1992).

The reader, alert to Darcy's strangled feelings for Elizabeth, will enjoy the **irony** of her carefree misreading of his behaviour in the park, and groan at Fitzwilliam's revelations about Darcy's role in separating Jane and Bingley, which is obviously going to obstruct or prevent the working out of their relationship. Later an indignant, angry Elizabeth speculates about the objections, which she deems snobbish prejudice against her relatives, mere lawyers and businessmen. She cries, gets a headache, and does not go to Rosings for tea.

STUDY FOCUS: PROPRIETY AND SOCIAL POSITION   A02

In Chapter XII (Chapter 35) we discover that Darcy is much more struck by Elizabeth's relations' 'want of propriety' (p. 193) than by their position in society. Elizabeth misjudges him in this chapter, ascribing to him more pride and snobbishness than he actually possesses: '*he* was the cause, his pride and caprice were the cause of all that Jane had suffered, and still continued to suffer' (p. 182). In focusing on what she perceives to be his prejudices, she reveals her own prejudice against him.

Later in the novel (Chapters XII, XVIII (Chapters 35, 41)) both Darcy and Mr Bennet claim that the elder Bennet girls can escape the restrictions and embarrassments of their family purely by means of their own praiseworthy behaviour. Class division – and the possible crossing of social boundaries that seem insurmountable – are **themes** of *Pride and Prejudice*. But here Elizabeth believes that Darcy's snobbery has prevailed so as to quash Jane's hopes of marriage with Bingley.

GRADE BOOSTER   A02

Define the **narrator**'s views of social division and snobbery by comparing Chapter X (Chapter 33) with other revealing episodes in *Pride and Prejudice*.

REVISION FOCUS: TASK 2   A03

How far do you agree with the following statements?

● Austen depicts family life in both positive and negative ways.
● The relationship between marriage and money is thoroughly explored in *Pride and Prejudice*.

Write opening paragraphs for essays based on these discussion points. Set out your arguments clearly.

VOLUME TWO, CHAPTER XI (CHAPTER 34)

SUMMARY

- Darcy tells Elizabeth of his love for her and, in doing so, dwells on the problem posed by her inferior social class.
- Darcy realises she is rejecting his proposal and asks her why she is so uncivil about it. Elizabeth charges him with ruining Jane's happiness, and tells him that she has disliked him since she heard about how he treated Wickham.
- Darcy fears that his mistake was to mention the very real social and financial obstacles to their match.
- Elizabeth accuses him of not behaving in a 'gentleman-like manner' (p. 188) and of being 'the last man in the world whom I could ever be prevailed on to marry' (p. 188).

COMMENTARY

ELIZABETH'S STATE OF MIND

Nursing her anger at Darcy's interference, Elizabeth re-examines all the letters that Jane has sent her 'as if intending to exasperate herself as much as possible against Mr Darcy' (p. 184). The letters lack Jane's characteristic 'cheerfulness' (p. 184). She consoles herself with the fact that Darcy is due to leave within two days and that within a fortnight she will see Jane again in London. She will be sorry to see Colonel Fitzwilliam leave but she knows from their discussion of money that he could never marry her.

When Darcy declares his love – 'You must allow me to tell you how ardently I admire and love you' (p. 185) – Elizabeth is silent. Darcy seems sure that Elizabeth will accept him but Elizabeth would have refused him even had his request been made differently. She is offended by his lack of tact, and treats him without much compassion: 'if I could *feel* gratitude, I would now thank you' (p. 186). Her manner of putting him down is consistent with Austen's creation of her as a feisty, witty and self-confident young woman. After the proposal, Elizabeth cries, 'The tumult of her mind … now painfully great' (p. 189). She is flattered that he should have asked her, but curses his 'abominable pride' (p. 189). She goes to her room in order not to have to meet Charlotte.

STUDY FOCUS: A PROPOSAL AND A REJECTION [A02]

Who is more in the wrong in this melodramatic scene? Darcy's bumbling explanations of what he had to overcome in order to allow himself to court Elizabeth, his strong sense of his own superior position in society, and his easy assumption that she will accept his hand, are all unsympathetic aspects of his proposal.

However, events prove that Elizabeth is rash to have trusted Wickham's account of Darcy, and her rejection of the proposal is spiced with self-righteous anger.

GRADE BOOSTER [A02]

Darcy's proposal appears at a strategic point, midway through the novel. From this point on, there are far fewer social ceremonies (balls, dinners, dances) and, instead, Elizabeth is to spend more time in reflection. Arriving slowly at private judgements will increasingly take the place of witty public display.

CHECK THE FILM [A04]

In the BBC version Darcy's proposal is thoroughly and convincingly offensive. How else could it be played?

GLOSSARY

189 **avowal** frank admission or acknowledgement

VOLUME TWO, CHAPTER XII (CHAPTER 35)

SUMMARY

- Elizabeth goes for a walk. She meets Darcy who hands her a letter which she reads 'with no expectation of pleasure, but with the strongest curiosity' (p. 191).
- In the letter, Darcy explains at length his conduct with Bingley and Wickham – 'my actions and their motives' (p. 191).
- Darcy closes his letter to Elizabeth with an assurance of the truth of his account.

ANALYSIS

DARCY ON JANE AND BINGLEY

In his letter, Darcy explains his belief that Jane was 'indifferent' (p. 192) to Bingley. He describes the problems posed by an association with the Bennet family: Mrs Bennet's low connections, but more the 'total lack of propriety so frequently, so almost uniformly betrayed by herself, your three younger sisters, and occasionally even by your father' (p. 193). The behaviour of all at the ball at Netherfield convinced him of the undesirability of the match. Thereafter, Darcy, encouraged by Bingley's sisters, joined Bingley in London and dissuaded him from marriage. He admits that he knew that Jane was in London and that he hid this knowledge from Bingley.

DARCY ON WICKHAM

Darcy describes Wickham's upbringing and the close relationship that existed between the late Darcy and his godson: 'My father was not only fond of this young man's society, whose manners were always engaging; he also had the highest opinion of him' (p. 194). Darcy senior paid for Wickham to go to Cambridge University and hoped to provide him with a career in the church. Darcy junior had never been as impressed with Wickham as his father was, seeing more at first hand of his 'vicious propensities' and 'want of principle' (p. 194) than Darcy senior ever could.

Darcy had the task of promoting Wickham's career and giving him a living and a legacy of a thousand pounds. Some six months later Wickham wrote to Darcy to inform him that he had no intention of following a career in the church. Darcy gave him the thousand pounds. Wickham renounced his claim to the living and was given an immediate pay-off of three thousand pounds. Darcy and Wickham heard nothing of each other for three years. Wickham then wrote to ask for the church living that he had refused, since his circumstances were now 'exceedingly bad' (p. 195). Darcy refused. Finally, during the preceding summer, Wickham tried to elope with Miss Darcy and was only just prevented by the intervention of Darcy.

STUDY FOCUS: DARCY THE LETTER-WRITER (A02)

In letters, as opposed to conversation, things can be written and explained that could never be spoken in a social situation. Letters can be studied and reread and the attitudes to the writer can mature and change. Darcy comments that he was not sufficiently 'master' (p. 197) of himself to reveal in conversation what he has put in the letter. He asserts that his 'character required it to be written and read' (p. 191). Darcy may not be much of a conversationalist, but he writes a strong and intelligent letter (as we learned in Volume One, Chapter X (Chapter 10)). Darcy's letter in this chapter is something of a bombshell so far as Elizabeth is concerned. In the next chapter we see what effect the process of reading and digesting his argument has on her.

CONTEXT (A04)

The 'living' rejected by Wickham is a benefice, an endowed post in the Church of England, with an income and property for its holder, which was in the gift of landowners like Darcy. Mr Bennet's message to Mr Collins in the final pages of the book – 'if I were you, I would stand by the nephew. He has more to give' (p. 362) – is a terse reminder of Darcy's power and patronage. Nowadays it seems extraordinary that church officials were as a matter of course appointed by the laity.

GLOSSARY

193	**censure**	expression of disapproval or criticism
193	**remonstrance**	forceful protest
194	**veracity**	truthfulness
194	**propensities**	inclinations or natural tendencies
195	**pecuniary**	relating to money
195	**dissipation**	wasteful expenditure, indulgence in pleasures

VOLUME TWO, CHAPTER XIII (CHAPTER 36)

SUMMARY

- On her first reading of the letter, convinced as she is of Darcy's guilt, Elizabeth is angered by his reference to her family and incredulous about his account of Wickham's behaviour.

- Elizabeth rereads the letter and realises that Darcy may be 'entirely blameless' (p. 199) in the affair. She is ashamed and regrets her prejudice.

- On her return to the parsonage, she discovers that Darcy and Fitzwilliam have both visited to pay their respects before leaving Kent.

ANALYSIS

ELIZABETH DIGESTS DARCY'S LETTER

Prompted by Darcy's letter to reassess his role in events, Elizabeth recalls that she had no knowledge of Wickham before being introduced to him and recognises the inappropriate way he told her his personal history on their second meeting: 'She was now struck with the impropriety of such communications to a stranger' (p. 200). She remembers that Wickham chose to avoid Darcy at the Netherfield ball, and that, after Bingley and Darcy had left the county, Wickham did not scruple to inform everybody of his situation. She now sees Wickham's attentions to Miss King in a different light as 'solely and hatefully mercenary' (p. 201) and questions the motives behind Wickham's attentions to herself.

She reads again Darcy's account of Jane and Bingley and realises that he could well have mistaken her reserve for want of feeling. She remembers the behaviour of the Bennets at the Netherfield ball (Volume One, Chapter XVIII (Chapter 18)) and acknowledges the justice in his comments on her family. She realises that she has been 'blind, partial, prejudiced, absurd' (p. 201) and feels humiliated. This chapter is central to the movement of the novel since it marks the turnaround in Elizabeth's opinion, and there are several references to the 'perturbed' (p. 199) workings of her mind 'giving way to every variety of thought' (p. 203) as she processes the letter.

STUDY FOCUS: READING AND REREADING   `A02`

In this description of Elizabeth's appraisal of the letter and its material, Austen provides us with a model for reading. To begin with, we read superficially and see only what we want, but rereading and rereading can result in a complete shift in all our perspectives. Here Elizabeth is forced to revise her attitudes and understanding; up until now, she has been misreading the situation. The reader also has to share this process of re-interpretation and realignment, going over the events of the novel to see whether, like Elizabeth, they have lacked the moral scrupulousness to see through Wickham, to judge Darcy fairly and to comprehend how much the Bennet family are lacking in propriety. Austen wants us also to struggle with these new implications.

VOLUME TWO, CHAPTERS XIV, XV AND XVI (CHAPTERS 37–9)

SUMMARY

- Lady Catherine summons Mr and Mrs Collins and their guests to Rosings. She tells Elizabeth that she should stay longer at the parsonage but Elizabeth says she must go.

- Elizabeth studies Darcy's letter and is unhappy. Lady Catherine's pomposity is a comic contrast to this new seriousness.

- Elizabeth and Maria Lucas leave to stay with the Gardiners in London. Elizabeth decides that she will not tell Jane anything concerning Bingley.

- Elizabeth and Maria travel back to Hertfordshire with Jane, where they are met by Lydia and Kitty. Lydia dominates the conversation. At home, Mrs Bennet is pleased to see her daughters and Mr Bennet stirs himself so far as to tell Elizabeth 'more than once' (p. 213) that he is glad that she has come home.

- Mrs Bennet presses her husband to allow her daughters to go to Brighton.

ANALYSIS

ELIZABETH'S MISERY

When Elizabeth is alone she studies Darcy's letter. The **narrator** shows how completely Elizabeth has come to believe in Darcy's letter, and what misery this brings her: 'In her own past behaviour, there was a constant source of vexation and regret' (p. 206). She does not regret having rejected him, but she is ashamed of the way in which she did it, and now feels some compassion for him. She is embarrassed by 'the unhappy defects of her family' (p. 206), in particular the propensity of Catherine and Lydia to flirt with officers, with their mother's encouragement. Above all Elizabeth is unhappy that 'the folly and indecorum of her own family' (p. 207) should have cost Jane her chance of happiness.

MR COLLINS

Mr Collins thanks Elizabeth for her visit with elaborate and long-winded formality, reminding her of the kindness she has received in the superior society of Lady Catherine. He boasts about the success of his marriage: 'We seem to have been designed for each other' (p. 209). Elizabeth is truly sorry to leave Charlotte.

So elaborate are Mr Collins's compliments that Austen runs the risk of boring the reader. The contrast between his self-satisfaction and Elizabeth's short replies is typical of this chapter. Elizabeth's attempts to 'unite civility and truth in a few short sentences' (p. 209) indicate a gulf between her private feelings and the trivial public conversation in which she has to participate.

STUDY FOCUS: LYDIA'S SPEECH A02

Lydia's speech is characterised by exclamations, **rhetorical questions**, incomplete sentences and invocations: 'Aye', 'Lord' (p. 181). Her speech is even more wild and digressive than that of her mother. She is loud and listens to no one, but she does have a youthful and vulgar vitality that is not to be ignored: 'Dear me! we had such a good piece of fun the other day at Colonel Forster's!' (p. 213) Here all Elizabeth's newly exacerbated fears about her family are confirmed. Lydia's anarchic fecklessness, the plan to stay in Brighton, and her father's refusal clearly to disallow it: all these are stark reminders of the impropriety that Darcy summed up in his letter.

VOLUME TWO, CHAPTER XVII (CHAPTER 40)

SUMMARY

- Elizabeth finally tells Jane about what has occurred between her and Darcy, omitting any reference to Jane and Bingley.

- Elizabeth realises that Jane is not happy and is still very much in love with Bingley.

- Mrs Bennet has given up any hope of Bingley marrying Jane. She asks Elizabeth about life at Hunsford Parsonage and about Charlotte's household management. She again expresses her bitterness at the entailment that will make Mr Collins the eventual owner of Longbourn.

ANALYSIS

WICKHAM'S TRUE CHARACTER

Jane is shocked by Elizabeth's revelations about Wickham: '"I do not know when I have been more shocked," said she. "Wickham so very bad! It is almost past belief"' (p. 217). She is all softness and compassion at Darcy's misery. However, when it comes to a discussion of whether Wickham's true nature should be more widely known, Jane is clear: 'Surely there can be no occasion for exposing him so dreadfully' (p. 218). The two sisters agree that 'Wickham will soon be gone; and it will not signify to anybody here, what he really is' (p. 218). Jane is also concerned that he might be sorry for what he has done and that his 'past errors' should not be allowed to 'ruin him for ever' (p. 218).

STUDY FOCUS: APPEARANCE AND REALITY (A02)

The discussion between Jane and Elizabeth in this chapter connects to a major **theme** of the novel, the discrepancy between appearance and reality, as made manifest in Darcy and Wickham: 'One has all the goodness, and the other all the appearance of it' (p. 217). While the sisters are broadly in agreement about the two men, Austen signals to readers some of the differences between them in their comments about both Darcy and Wickham. For example, Jane says that she 'never thought Mr Darcy so deficient in the *appearance* of [goodness] as you used to do' (p. 217) and Elizabeth criticises herself for being 'weak and vain and nonsensical' (p. 218) in her dealings with them. Learning in this way that 'an expression of goodness' (p. 217) does not always signify a virtuous nature has perturbed both sisters, particularly Elizabeth.

KEY QUOTATION: VOLUME TWO, CHAPTER XVII (CHAPTER 40) (A01)

Key quotation: 'One may be continually abusive without saying any thing just; but one cannot always be laughing at a man without now and then stumbling on something witty' (p. 218).

- Elizabeth shows great self-knowledge here as she admits that a comment that is 'witty' may be far from 'just'.

- She reproaches herself for treating Darcy unfairly and seems to suggest that her behaviour showed a want of modesty and good judgement on her part.

- While her tone here is more good-humoured than distressed, her sentiments are similar to those expressed in Chapter XIII (Chapter 36): '"How despicably I have acted!" she cried. – "I, who have prided myself on my discernment!"'

GRADE BOOSTER (A02)

Mrs Bennet enquires after Elizabeth's opinion of 'this sad business of Jane's' (p. 219) but the conversation is dominated by Mrs Bennet's views on the matter. We are reminded that Mrs Bennet's views have not undergone any changes, unlike those of her two eldest daughters. As readers, we are also now privy to Darcy's critical comments about the Bennet family and may find ourselves viewing the Bennets in a more critical light.

CHECK THE BOOK (A03)

Written around a century later than *Pride and Prejudice*, Charlotte Perkins Gilman's novella *The Yellow Wallpaper* (1892) also deals with the themes of marriage and of the lives of upper-class women but themes of madness and confinement make it a very different depiction of a woman's struggles against convention.

VOLUME TWO, CHAPTER XVIII (CHAPTER 41)

SUMMARY

- The regiment is to leave in a week's time, making Kitty and Lydia miserable. They still hope to go to Brighton. Elizabeth is ashamed of their behaviour and remembers Darcy's objections with understanding.
- Lydia is invited to Brighton. Elizabeth advises her father not to let her go, considering the invitation 'as the death-warrant of all possibility of common sense' (p. 222) for Lydia.
- Elizabeth meets Wickham several times before the departure of the regiment.
- Lydia leaves for Brighton. Kitty weeps 'with vexation and envy' (p. 227).

ANALYSIS

ELIZABETH'S FEARS

Elizabeth secretly advises Mr Bennet not to allow Lydia to go. She tells him in the strongest terms that Lydia's imprudent behaviour is detrimental to them all. Mr Bennet ironically attributes her intervention to self-concern: 'What, has she frightened away some of your lovers?' (p. 223). When Mr Bennet sees how serious Elizabeth is he explains his belief that Colonel Forster will control Lydia and that she will be of less account in Brighton, which may do her good: 'The officers will find women better worth their notice' (p. 224).

Though he starts by mocking Elizabeth, her new seriousness causes Mr Bennet to lower his defences. He expresses real admiration for Jane and Elizabeth and says that they 'will not appear to less advantage for having a couple of – or I may say, three very silly sisters' (p. 223). He shows by his explanation that he has at least given the matter of Lydia's folly some thought.

LYDIA'S IMAGINATION

This is a very varied chapter that contains stark opposites of behaviour and feeling. In a strange passage unlike anything else in the book, the **narrator** enters Lydia's 'imagination' and shows the vision of Brighton she has constructed 'with the creative eye of fancy' (p. 224). Her fantasy, in which 'she saw herself seated beneath a tent, tenderly flirting with at least six officers at once' (p. 224), accords with Elizabeth's description of her as 'A flirt … in the worst and meanest degree of flirtation' (p. 223). The contrast between Lydia's fevered excitement and Elizabeth's eloquent anger could not be greater.

STUDY FOCUS: APPEARANCE AND REALITY A02

We are reminded in this chapter of Jane and Elizabeth's discussion in the preceding chapter, and that appearance and reality is a **theme** examined throughout the book.

Elizabeth shows her strength and moral purpose with Wickham, whom she now sees as affected and dishonest. He is left not quite knowing where he stands with her – does she know the truth about his past? She states that Darcy 'improves on acquaintance' (p. 225), but Wickham says he is pleased that Darcy is 'wise enough to assume even the *appearance* of what is right' (p. 226). Picking up the word, the narrator comments on Wickham's continued appearance of 'usual cheerfulness' (p. 226), though he is obviously rattled. Lydia's fantasy of Brighton is based also all on appearance. The underlying moral reality is presented in Elizabeth's grim view.

VOLUME TWO, CHAPTER XIX (CHAPTER 42)

SUMMARY

- Mr Bennet's marriage is explained and Elizabeth's anxieties about his irresponsible behaviour are explored.

- Elizabeth looks forward to her visit to the Lakes with the Gardiners, though is sad that Jane is not able to accompany them. Elizabeth takes cynical solace in the fact that as the holiday plan is not quite perfect, she is less likely to be disappointed by it. Lydia writes hurried and infrequent letters.

- Mrs Gardiner writes with a revised plan – to go only as far as Derbyshire and to visit the places in which she used to live. Elizabeth is very disappointed. She cannot think of Derbyshire without thinking of Darcy and Pemberley.

- Elizabeth and the Gardiners find themselves in the small village of Lambton, some five miles away from Pemberley. Mrs Gardiner longs to visit Pemberley but Elizabeth dreads meeting Darcy. However, after finding out that he is absent, she agrees to accompany her aunt.

ANALYSIS

THE BENNETS' MARRIAGE

The narrator explains the background to Mr Bennet's marriage. He fell in love with his wife's youth and beauty, overlooking her 'weak understanding and illiberal mind' (p. 228), and soon lost any love for her. He has devoted his life to reading, and finds in Mrs Bennet a source of amusement and little more. Elizabeth concedes that her father's behaviour has been irresponsible, especially where 'preserv[ing] the respectability of his daughters' (p. 229) is concerned.

STUDY FOCUS: MR BENNET   A02

Spanning six weeks or so between Lydia's leaving and Elizabeth's summer tour, this chapter imparts general information mixed with amusing circumstantial detail. It is odd that Austen has delayed the explanation of the unhappiness in Mr Bennet's marriage, and his refuge in the countryside, books and the ironic consolations of the 'true philosopher' (p. 228). However, these insights follow on naturally from Elizabeth's vain attempt to advise her father, and spell out her attitude to him and her view that the 'direction of his talents' has been 'ill-judged' (p. 229). She is grateful for his affection and respectful of his abilities, but has to strive to forget 'that continual breach of conjugal obligation and decorum which, in exposing his wife to the contempt of her own children, was so highly reprehensible' (p. 228). The severe abstraction of this kind of commentary (the way it deals with ideas rather than actual events) is sharpened by contrast with Lydia's distasteful letters.

CHECK THE BOOK   A03

Weak fathers are common in Austen's novels: Mr Woodhouse in *Emma* (1816) and Sir Walter Elliot in *Persuasion* (1818) are other examples.

CRITICAL VIEWPOINT   A03

It is essential for our belief in Elizabeth's good faith that she has no responsibility for the decision to visit Pemberley, otherwise it might look as if she has set out to capture Darcy. Instead the narrator stresses how much Elizabeth really wanted to go to the Lakes, how unwilling she is to visit Pemberley, and how careful she is to ascertain that Darcy is not in residence.

GLOSSARY

231   **petrified spars** specimens of fossilised wood

VOLUME THREE, CHAPTER 1 (CHAPTER 43)

CONTEXT A03

In the original format of the novel, the second volume finished with Chapter 42 and the third volume began with Chapter 43.

SUMMARY

- The Gardiners and Elizabeth visit Pemberley. Elizabeth reflects that 'to be mistress of Pemberley might be something!' (p. 235), and cannot help wondering what it might have been like to live there.
- They are shown about the house by Mrs Reynolds, the housekeeper.
- Darcy appears and treats them with surprising civility.
- Darcy tells Elizabeth that Bingley and his sisters are about to arrive. He asks if he may introduce his sister Georgiana to Elizabeth.
- On the way home Elizabeth's aunt and uncle praise Darcy but Mrs Gardiner, still believing Wickham has been Darcy's victim, continues to talk about Wickham and to compare the two men. Elizabeth relates an abbreviated version of the true relationship between them.

ANALYSIS

MRS REYNOLDS'S TOUR

The housekeeper Mrs Reynolds is delighted to talk about her master, Darcy. Elizabeth is surprised to discover that Darcy is considered by his servant to be anything but proud. 'To my fancy, it is only because he does not rattle away like other young men' (p. 239), says the housekeeper on this matter. Mrs Reynolds claims never to have heard a cross word from him and vouches for his kindness to his tenants, to the poor and to his sister. Elizabeth is amazed: '"In what an amiable light does this place him!" thought Elizabeth' (p. 239). Austen points out that it is the high esteem in which Mrs Reynolds holds Darcy the man rather than a more material interest in Darcy's beautiful home that provokes Elizabeth's admiration: 'Mrs Reynolds could interest her on no other point. She related the subject of the pictures, the dimensions of the rooms, and the price of the furniture, in vain' (p. 239). Austen is perhaps also conveying in this remark the extent of Elizabeth's astonishment at hearing 'this fine account of him' (p. 239).

THE DESCRIPTION OF PEMBERLEY

CONTEXT A04

It is believed that Jane Austen based Pemberley on Chatsworth House in Derbyshire. Search online for 'Chatsworth' or 'landscape gardens' to gain some impression of what Darcy's estate was like.

In Volume One, Chapter VIII (Chapter 8), when the conversation turned to Pemberley, Elizabeth had put down her book to listen. It is clearly supposed to be a famous country house, and the **narrator** describes the picturesque scenery and the house – 'a large, handsome, stone building, standing well on rising ground' (p. 235) – in more exact detail and at greater length than she does any other house or park in the novel. It is rather an abstract and frigid description (there are no **metaphors** to make it come alive), but it is a coherent and whole picture. The way it merges with the natural features without any appearance of artificiality is in line with contemporary aesthetics of the country house: 'She had never seen a place for which nature had done more, or where natural beauty had been so little counteracted by an awkward taste' (p. 235). It may also offer an implicit key to Darcy's character: there is more robust naturalness in him than artifice.

STUDY FOCUS: ELIZABETH AT PEMBERLEY A02

The visit to Pemberley is seen through Elizabeth's perceptions. She is very curious to see the house, is agitated as they enter Pemberley Woods and allows herself almost to feel regret that she is not its mistress. She is surprised and impressed by the housekeeper's love for her master and 'longed to hear more' (p. 238). She is allowing a different view of Darcy to replace her original assumptions about his arrogance and bad temper.

After Darcy's appearance she is flustered and embarrassed – she knows she should not be found visiting the house of a man whose offer of marriage she has rebuffed – but she still manages to watch him to see how he reacts. She cannot understand why he is being so polite – he 'spoke to Elizabeth, if not in terms of perfect composure, at least of perfect civility' (p. 241) – and her curiosity is extreme. During this chapter her feelings towards Darcy start to change, not least when he asks if he might introduce his sister to her. This is a great honour and seems proof that Darcy can feel no resentment towards her. Pemberley forces Elizabeth to start imagining what kind of person Darcy really is. Only a few shreds of her prejudice remain.

The reader feels a certain amusement in seeing Elizabeth undergo her emotional *volte-face* (turning round to face in the opposite direction). This comedy is underlined by Elizabeth's desire to keep the whole business a secret from her aunt and uncle. The **dramatic irony** caused by Elizabeth's keeping her relationship with Darcy a secret remains almost until the novel's end.

GRADE BOOSTER A02

Examine the many examples of secrecy in *Pride and Prejudice*, and place them in the moral framework that the book defines.

CHECK THE FILM A04

The BBC version of Elizabeth's meeting with Darcy in the grounds of Pemberley offers a striking and memorable departure from the text for visual effect. We see him just emerging from swimming in his lake, and his wet, dishevelled appearance is quite unlike the Darcy we have seen before. From now onwards in this adaptation he is a softer, less haughty and much more attractive character.

REVISION FOCUS: TASK 3 A03

How far do you agree with the following statements?

- Pemberley is presented to the reader very differently to the other homes in the novel.
- The reader has intimate access to Elizabeth's thoughts and feelings throughout the novel and consequently is more sympathetic towards her than towards Darcy.

Write opening paragraphs for essays based on these discussion points. Set out your arguments clearly.

VOLUME THREE, CHAPTERS II AND III (CHAPTERS 44 AND 45)

SUMMARY

- Miss Darcy and Bingley visit the Gardiners, who begin to imagine that Darcy may be partial to their niece. Elizabeth is very agitated and keen to please Miss Darcy.

- Darcy continues to be pleasant, and Elizabeth wonders at his kindness towards her aunt and uncle. Darcy asks his sister to invite the Gardiners and Elizabeth to Pemberley for dinner.

- Elizabeth realises that Darcy is probably still in love with her, and wonders whether she should try to encourage him to renew his addresses, which she thinks she has the 'power' (p. 253) to do.

- Mrs Gardiner and Elizabeth arrive at Pemberley and are received by Miss Darcy. Miss Bingley is jealous of Elizabeth and irritated to see that Darcy is doing all he can to make his sister and Elizabeth acquainted.

ANALYSIS

FALLING IN LOVE

The focus shifts occasionally away from Elizabeth to the Gardiners in Chapter II (Chapter 44). From watching her and Darcy, they have quickly arrived at 'the full conviction that one of them at least knew what it was to love. Of the lady's sensations they remained a little in doubt' (p. 249). Most of the chapter, however, deals with Elizabeth's reactions to Darcy's behaviour which has become 'so desirous to please, so free from self-consequence' (p. 251). Elizabeth spends as much time watching Bingley for signs of his continued love for Jane as she does keeping an eye on Darcy, and she observes 'no look' between Miss Darcy and Bingley 'that spoke particular regard' (p. 250).

At night, however, she thinks over the day's events and realises that she is grateful to Darcy for forgiving 'all the petulance and acrimony of her manner in rejecting him' (p. 253). She feels that such a change in him can only be attributed to 'love, ardent love' (p. 253). The discovery that Darcy's sixteen-year-old sister Georgiana is not proud but shy provides Elizabeth with another clue to Darcy's character. Embarrassment and shyness colour all their encounters from now until Darcy proposes again. They discuss this in Chapter XVIII (Chapter 60).

STUDY FOCUS: CAROLINE BINGLEY'S JEALOUSY **A02**

The jealous malice of Caroline Bingley and her interesting inability to control herself run throughout this chapter. She has nothing to gain from her rudeness to Elizabeth which she should see will only annoy Darcy but, as the **narrator** remarks, 'angry people are not always wise' (p. 259). She is unable to prevent herself from goading him until she hears him praise Elizabeth and feels hurt. Such malice combined with curiosity is a particular trial to Elizabeth, and then to Darcy.

Miss Bingley, like Lady Catherine later, achieves exactly the opposite of her intention. Rather than turning Darcy against Elizabeth, it brings the two of them together in the mutual knowledge of a shared secret (Miss Darcy's near elopement with Wickham), embarrasses Darcy and forces him to make public his admiration for Elizabeth, considering her to be 'one of the handsomest women of my acquaintance' (p. 259).

CHECK THE BOOK   **A04**

For a discussion of the depiction of Pemberley and wider aspects of the picturesque, see Isobel Armstrong's 'Politics, Pride, Prejudice and the Picturesque' in the *New Casebook* collection of essays on *Pride and Prejudice*, edited by Robert Clark (1984).

GRADE BOOSTER   **A02**

Is Caroline Bingley's behaviour the only example of deliberate malice in *Pride and Prejudice*? Are Elizabeth or the narrator ever malicious in their stinging remarks about other people?

GLOSSARY

248   **curricle** a type of open carriage with two wheels

VOLUME THREE, CHAPTER IV (CHAPTER 46)

SUMMARY

- Letters from Jane arrive to tell Elizabeth that Lydia has run away with Wickham but that he does not intend to marry her.
- Colonel Forster has tried to pursue them, but to no avail, and Jane begs Elizabeth to ask Mr Gardiner if he will help their father in London – Mr Bennet's 'excessive distress will not allow him to pursue any measure in the best and safest way' (p. 262).
- Darcy visits and hears this news. He is alarmed by how ill Elizabeth looks and comforts her as well as he can before leaving.
- The Gardiners hear the news and resolve to leave for Longbourn immediately with Elizabeth.

ANALYSIS

NEWS OF THE ELOPEMENT

In Jane's first letter, she writes that Lydia has run away to Scotland with Wickham. She is 'willing to hope the best' (p. 260) of the match, and believes that Wickham must be in love with Lydia since he knows that she will bring him no money. The second letter, written a day later, conveys the family fear that Lydia and Wickham do not intend marriage, but are 'living in sin'. Lydia had never seemed particularly interested in Wickham, but Elizabeth recognises that she was ready to attach herself to anyone, and that her virtue is not to be relied upon: 'she had no difficulty in believing that neither her virtue nor her understanding would preserve her from falling an easy prey' (p. 266). Elizabeth assumes that this latest family disgrace will dispel any love that Darcy might have felt for her.

STUDY FOCUS: MELODRAMA `A02`

This is a **melodramatic** episode in the novel with characters' agitation extremely evident, for example in Jane's hurried and scrawled letter and Elizabeth's trembling knees and 'breathless … accent' (p. 263). However, several shifts of focus bring intelligence to what could have been no more than sensational. Notably, Elizabeth is torn between a generalised concern for Lydia and her family, and a specific anxiety about what effect this will have on Darcy's apparent interest in her. The disgrace Lydia has brought on the family must be just the kind of vulgarity of which he most disapproves. By a terrible **irony** of the kind Austen seems to enjoy, just at the moment when it seems all must be over with Darcy, Elizabeth discovers that she has fallen in love with him: 'never had she so honestly felt that she could have loved him, as now, when all love must be vain' (p. 264).

CONTEXT `A04`

Up until 1856 Scottish law allowed marriage on the basis simply of a mutual declaration of willingness by both parties in front of a witness, without licence, banns or a priest. Gretna, just across the English border north of Carlisle, thus became the traditional venue for elopers and runaways, who could be wed by the blacksmith, no questions asked.

CHECK THE BOOK `A03`

The portrayal of human consciousness, as illustrated in Austen's showing of events through Elizabeth's mind, becomes one of the great themes of the European novel, reaching its most complete expression in the work of Henry James (1843–1916), James Joyce (1882–1941) and Virginia Woolf (1882–1941), and in French, the huge masterpiece of Marcel Proust (1871–1922), *A la recherche du temps perdu* (13 volumes, 1913–28).

GLOSSARY

262 **exigence** crisis, predicament

EXTENDED COMMENTARY

VOLUME THREE, CHAPTER IV (CHAPTER 46), PP. 264–6

There is nothing comic in the language of this passage, though the situation is full of heavy **irony**, perhaps one that has some psychological basis. The moment at which Elizabeth finds that she 'honestly' (p. 265) has started to love Darcy coincides with her almost certainly losing him as a result of the latest Bennet family disaster. Another irony – this might be comic, though again it seems wholly credible – is the discrepancy between what passes in the heart and mind of our heroine and (according to his reactions) in Darcy too, and their politeness to each other. Neither of them is so overwhelmed as to forget the nicety of apologising for not fulfilling their social engagements. It is still important to appear reasonable and polite even in such trying circumstances.

GRADE BOOSTER A02

Note how many abstract terms are used in the account of Elizabeth's feelings. See **Structure, Form and language** on p. 93.

The elopement of Lydia is indeed a **melodramatic** event, though one that has been carefully prepared for. It is a 'wretched, mistake' (p. 264) that Elizabeth did not publicise the wickedness of Wickham. She and Jane had discussed the matter, and decided against it, in Volume Two, Chapter XVII (Chapter 40), as the militia was just leaving Meryton. Had Elizabeth made public her knowledge of Wickham, her family might have been protected from this disaster. We will discover as the novel progresses that Darcy also blames himself for concealing Wickham's true character. Wickham's intrigue with Georgiana remains a shared secret between Elizabeth and Darcy throughout the whole second half of the novel. On the one hand, Austen seems to be arguing for a greater honesty about sexual mores, or, at least, about the dishonourable behaviour of male scoundrels; on the other hand, the indiscretions of a young girl should be wholly sealed from public notice.

Although in the twenty-first century we generally have different ideas about sexual behaviour and morality, we can still empathise with the tragic consequence of Austen's sub-plot – that 'Lydia's infamy' (p. 266) will cause her to be 'lost for ever' (p. 264). The way Austen writes about Lydia's running away suggests a double view about possible sexual relations before marriage. If the couple marry, their indiscretion may be ignored or eventually forgotten. If they do not marry, the woman's future is in jeopardy, while the man may probably carry on as he pleases. Once again in *Pride and Prejudice*, albeit in particularly unfavourable circumstances, marriage is the central concern of our protagonists.

Primogeniture, the right of the eldest son to inherit property, title and power to the exclusion of all others – a social system likely to value the virginity of brides – is always in the background of *Pride and Prejudice*. Colonel Fitzwilliam is the typical younger brother: 'younger sons cannot marry where they like' (p. 179). Wickham passes himself off as a similarly disappointed male, cheated by the power of the favoured heir (though, of course, without any justification). The entail, a result of the view that only males should inherit property, hovers over the Bennet women. The possession of money and power, inherited wealth and property, or the lack of such privileges, are of the most acute significance in the society Austen depicts. It is bad enough that Lydia has thrown herself away on someone with neither wealth nor the diligence required for a career. Worse is Elizabeth's certainty, which is expressed soon after this passage, that Wickham has no intention of marrying Lydia.

GRADE BOOSTER A02

Why does Austen feel the necessity for authorial commentary in these passages, rather than allowing the action to speak for itself?

Towards the end of the passage there are two sentences of peculiarly heavy authorial commentary on the significance of Elizabeth's 'change of sentiment' (p. 265). The **narrator** questions whether 'gratitude and esteem', the basis for Elizabeth's new feelings for Darcy, are sufficient and proper and shows a dual concern for psychological realism and morality ('neither improbable … nor faulty') in thinking about Elizabeth's change. Then, in a curiously awkward construction, 'gratitude and esteem' are compared with another kind of affection, 'what is so often described as arising on a first interview with its object, and even before two words can be exchanged' (p. 265): in other words, love at first sight (or, at least, sexual attraction). Although the narrator ironically describes this as the more 'interesting mode of attachment' (p. 266), love based on appearance and immediate sexual attraction is perhaps not to be trusted, suggests the narrator, at least not by Elizabeth. Her 'partiality for Wickham' (p. 265), built on the immediate impression of his charming manner, on outward appearances, met with 'ill-success' (p. 266).

One wonders why Austen, who can be so linguistically clever, hedges and complicates this narratorial comment with 'if', 'but' and 'otherwise', and such awkward **circumlocutions**. Is this heavy humour, or a wish to discuss in a guarded way the key **thematic** interest in different modes of love? Having made Elizabeth detest Darcy for half the novel, now she has to explain the way in which her heroines's mind has been changed by such unglamorous feelings as 'gratitude and esteem'.

VOLUME THREE, CHAPTERS V AND VI (CHAPTERS 47 AND 48)

SUMMARY

- At Longbourn there is no news of Lydia. Mrs Gardiner is puzzled as to what secret information Elizabeth seems to have about Wickham. Once again Elizabeth regrets not having made public her knowledge of Wickham's true character.
- Elizabeth sees Lydia's letter. Mr Bennet, never a good correspondent, has not written, and Mr Gardiner leaves to join him in London.
- Elizabeth hears that Mrs Philips and Lady Lucas have visited Longbourn in the past week. The whole of Meryton is full of stories of Wickham's debts and seductions.
- Mr Collins sends a letter suggesting that Mr Bennet disown Lydia.
- Mr Gardiner has had no success trying to trace Wickham's family or friends. Mr Bennet comes home. There is still no news of the 'fugitives' (p. 272).

ANALYSIS

LYDIA'S LETTER

Elizabeth is shown Lydia's note explaining her departure. She describes the 'good joke' (p. 276) of breaking the news of her marriage to her family and gloats about how she will soon sign her name 'Lydia Wickham' (p. 276). Elizabeth is shocked by her 'thoughtless, thoughtless' (p. 277) sister, but consoled to think that it appears that it was at least Lydia's sincere intention to marry Wickham in Gretna Green.

STUDY FOCUS: REACTIONS TO LYDIA'S DISGRACE $\quad$ A02

The various family reactions to Lydia's disgrace are contrasted in Chapter V (Chapter 47). Jane is optimistic and tries to see the best in everyone. The Gardiners are cautiously helpful and concerned. Mrs Bennet blames everyone but herself, and is torn between worrying what clothes Lydia will buy in London and fantasising about her husband fighting with Wickham – 'and then he will be killed, and what is to become of us all?' (p. 273). Mr Bennet has converted his shock into silence, and has only written one short note from London. Mary delivers a sermon on the fragility of female virtue, preaching 'that one false step involves her in endless ruin' (p. 275). Elizabeth keeps her intelligence and **irony** at play, fully conscious of the worst that is likely to have happened to Lydia, but irritated by neighbours' curiosity, remarking that 'under such a misfortune as this, one cannot see too little of one's neighbours' (p. 278).

Mr Collins's letter in Chapter VI (Chapter 48) is grotesquely callous – 'The death of your daughter would have been a blessing in comparison of this' (p. 281) – though it pretends to sympathy – 'you are grievously to be pitied' (p. 282). He even comments that his rejection by Elizabeth has in retrospect been a lucky escape 'for had it been otherwise, I must have been involved in all your sorrow and disgrace' (p. 282). The reader may wonder why Austen gives the most hypocritical and uncharitable view of the situation to a clergyman.

For his own part, Mr Bennet accepts the blame for Lydia's behaviour – 'It has been my own doing, and I ought to feel it' – while acknowledging that his feelings of guilt and shame will 'pass away soon enough' (p. 284). Even when admitting his responsibility for Lydia's misbehaviour to Elizabeth, he still retains an **ironic** detachment that the reader may choose to find either sympathetically amusing or somewhat shockingly disengaged from the grim reality of the situation.

CONTEXT $\quad$ A04

Mrs Bennet's idea that her husband will challenge Wickham to a duel is clearly absurd. However, duelling was not that uncommon at the time, especially in the army. In 1809 two prominent Tory Cabinet Ministers, George Canning (Foreign Secretary) and Viscount Castlereagh (Secretary for War), fought a duel with pistols which was widely reported in the newspapers. In Britain, a military law of 1844 made the activity illegal in the army, and thereafter the practice died away.

GRADE BOOSTER $\quad$ A02

Examine in detail the portrayal of Mr Bennet in Chapter VI (Chapter 48). How does the **narrator** shape our view of him?

GLOSSARY

273	**terrific**	dreadful
279	**dilatory**	slow to act

VOLUME THREE, CHAPTER VII (CHAPTER 49)

SUMMARY

- Mr Gardiner writes that Lydia and Wickham have been found but are not yet married. An arrangement has, however, been settled and Lydia is to be married from the Gardiners' home.
- Mr Bennet is reluctant to reply, realising that Wickham's acceptance of Lydia must have involved a large sum of money.
- Mrs Bennet is overjoyed that one daughter is at last to be married and immediately begins to think about wedding clothes.

ANALYSIS

THE FINANCIAL ARRANGEMENT

Mr Bennet shows a proper concern that he will not be able repay his brother-in-law whatever large sum must have been offered to Wickham so that 'there will be some little money, even when all his debts are discharged, to settle on my niece' (p. 286). This is contrasted with Mrs Bennet's unreflecting delight in Lydia's prospective marriage. The superficiality of Mrs Bennet's response is compounded by her thoughtless and selfish lack of concern for her brother's generosity, which she dismisses as simply what is due from him: 'It is the first time we have ever had any thing from him, except a few presents' (p. 290). This superficiality contrasts with the understanding and tact, not to mention generosity, that Mr Gardiner, her brother, has demonstrated throughout this ordeal.

STUDY FOCUS: LYDIA AND HER MOTHER A02

Mrs Bennet is linked to Lydia by their lack of moral reflection and their shared obsession with clothes. We may recall how in Volume Two, Chapter XVI (Chapter 39), Lydia bought a bonnet with the money intended for the sisters' lunch, and here, Mrs Bennet can barely wait to place 'some very plentiful orders' of 'calico, muslin, and cambric' (p. 290) despite the 'obligations which Mr Gardiner's behaviour laid them all under' (p. 290). Austen uses the **motif** as a way of indicating the worst excesses of female silliness; Jane and Elizabeth, in contrast, seem little interested in fashion or drapery and show a great deal more wisdom and realism than their mother in their reading of the situation.

KEY QUOTATION: VOLUME THREE, CHAPTER VII (CHAPTER 49) A01

Key quotation: '"And are they really to be married!" cried Elizabeth, as soon as they were by themselves. "How strange this is! And for *this* we are to be thankful. That they should marry, small as is their chance of happiness, and wretched as is his character, we are forced to rejoice! Oh, Lydia!"' (p. 288)

- Elizabeth's exclamations offer a commentary on events that the reader may share: that this is a happier outcome than it might have been but one that seems 'strange' and worrying. Elizabeth is concerned that a foundation for a happy future together has not been established by this union.
- Though the circumstances are very different, the reader may draw a parallel with Elizabeth's anxieties about the future married life of her friend Charlotte Lucas.
- Jane's and Elizabeth's own prospects in love and marriage have receded into the background during the last few chapters. As the novel approaches its end, will there be marriages to make the reader truly 'rejoice'?

CHECK THE FILM A04

The BBC version of *Pride and Prejudice*, typical of the 'costume drama' genre, offers the viewer a spectacular fashion parade of dresses, bonnets and other adornments, some garish and unflattering to a modern way of thinking. Austen herself associates an obsessive interest in fashion with folly.

CONTEXT A04

This chapter begins with a fleeting reference to Mrs Hill, the housekeeper at Longbourn, and also to the family's butler. Housekeepers were in charge of the entire female staff in a household and, in a small household, a butler would have been the head of the male staff. Larger households would have also employed a steward, the head of all staff.

GLOSSARY

288 **distressed himself** i.e. financially

VOLUME THREE, CHAPTER VIII (CHAPTER 50)

SUMMARY

- Mr Bennet approves Mr Gardiner's suggestions.
- Elizabeth realises that she loves Darcy.
- Lydia wishes to visit before she leaves, and, thanks to the efforts of Jane and Elizabeth, their father gives his permission. It is arranged that the newly-wed couple will come to Longbourn after the wedding ceremony.

GRADE BOOSTER **A02**

Relate the different kinds of interest that characters display towards wealth and status to the larger moral preoccupations of *Pride and Prejudice*.

ANALYSIS

THE BENNETS' FINANCES

Austen gives precise details of the financial arrangements. We learn that Mr Bennet will 'scarcely be ten pounds a-year the loser' (p. 293) with the settlement on Lydia. His irresponsibility as a father is exemplified by the absence of financial provision for his daughters, exposing them to the realities of the marriage market. Other novels by Austen feature similar incompetent father figures, though Mr Gardiner is a model of domestic responsibility.

ELIZABETH AND DARCY

Elizabeth begins to wish that she had never told Darcy about Lydia's disgrace. She reflects bitterly that there is very little chance of Darcy ever wanting to connect himself in any way to Wickham – 'a man whom he so justly scorned' (p. 295). She realises that she now thinks of Darcy as the perfect husband for herself and views their union as one that would have been improving for both of them: 'by her ease and liveliness, his mind might have been softened, his manners improved, and from his judgment, information, and knowledge of the world, she must have received benefit of greater importance' (p. 295). Where once she dwelt on Darcy's flaws, she now celebrates his qualities. Elizabeth draws an interesting contrast between the model of 'connubial felicity' (p. 296) her own marriage to Darcy might have been and the hastily arranged marriage of Wickham and Lydia 'who were only brought together because their passions were stronger than their virtue' (p. 296).

GLOSSARY

296 **the regulars** whereas the militia were a mobile military force, the 'regulars' had fixed camps throughout the country

296 **ensigncy** an ensign was the lowest grade of commissioned officer in an infantry regiment

STUDY FOCUS: MR AND MRS BENNET **A02**

The contrast established in the last chapter between Mr Bennet's anger and anxiety over what has happened and Mrs Bennet's inability to grasp the financial and moral realities of Lydia's behaviour is brought to a head here. Mr Bennet has been given much food for thought by his brother-in-law's endeavours on his family's behalf and feels concern and regret. This is, however, tempered by his characteristic indolence; ultimately the 'trifling exertion' (p. 293) of one hundred pounds per annum comes as a 'welcome surprise' (p. 293).

Mrs Bennet's reactions are far less nuanced for she 'was more alive to the disgrace, which the want of new clothes must reflect on her daughter's nuptials, than to any sense of shame at her eloping and living with Wickham' (p. 294). The outcome is for her 'a triumph' (p. 294) and her reaction to her husband's anger uncomprehending. Her only regret appears to be that Lydia will no longer be in regular contact with the young men of the militia and views her new quarters in the north as a kind of banishment.

VOLUME THREE, CHAPTERS IX AND X (CHAPTERS 51 AND 52)

SUMMARY

- Lydia and Wickham arrive and are to stay for ten days. Elizabeth discovers from Lydia that Darcy was present at their wedding. She writes to Mrs Gardiner to find out more.
- Mrs Gardiner's long letter describes Darcy's pivotal role in bringing about Lydia's wedding, including paying Wickham a large sum to marry her, and suggests Darcy's motivation for this.
- Elizabeth regrets the impossibility of ever marrying Darcy.
- She encounters Wickham, who asks her about her visit to Pemberley. Elizabeth shows that she knows more about his behaviour than he thinks.

ANALYSIS

PLEASURE AND PAIN

After reading Mrs Gardiner's letter Elizabeth is overcome by a storm of thoughts 'in which it was difficult to determine whether pleasure or pain bore the greatest share' (p. 308). She is fully aware of the enormous obligation that she and her family now bear Darcy, regrets ever having treated him badly, and is proud of the nobility of his behaviour. Even though 'Her heart did whisper, that he had done it for her' (p. 308), it is a short-lived thought. But on this subject, the reader more readily sides with Mrs Gardiner than with Elizabeth. Our sense of the comic texture and structure of the novel makes it reassuringly likely that Darcy's doings are prompted by his continued interest in Elizabeth. Yet for Elizabeth, it is impossible for her to imagine that Darcy would be prepared to be the brother-in-law of Wickham.

ELIZABETH'S USE OF LANGUAGE

Elizabeth's verbal fencing with Wickham is an interesting example of how strong and intelligent she is, and how necessary in Austen's world it is to use language to take control of a situation. She makes clear by hints and allusions that she knows all there is to know about Wickham's wrongdoing in the past; for example, 'How should you have liked making sermons?' (p. 310) is a knowing enquiry masquerading as an innocent one. She takes some pleasure in leaving him suitably embarrassed, while at the same time retaining that surface of politeness suitable to a sister-in-law.

STUDY FOCUS: LYDIA AND WICKHAM   A02

The appearance of Lydia and Wickham in the family circle is depicted dramatically, and without authorial comment. Jane and Elizabeth's amazement at their impudence is comment enough, along with Elizabeth's sharp rebuke of Lydia's crass offer to find suitors for her sisters: 'I do not particularly like your way of getting husbands' (p. 300). Meanwhile Mrs Bennet is all thoughtless pleasure at seeing her favourite daughter again and Mr Bennet is coldly and quietly angry. Despite everything, we also hear of sisterly concern from Elizabeth towards Lydia; she observes a troubling if predictable imbalance between Wickham's affection for her sister and Lydia's for him.

GRADE BOOSTER **A02**

What part do Lydia's folly and bad behaviour play in advancing the plot of *Pride and Prejudice* and bringing about its happy conclusion?

CHECK THE BOOK **A03**

Elizabeth's need to arrive at a dignified and civilised relationship with Wickham represents a particular view of human behaviour that Austen seems to value. How different this is from the wild and remorseless hatreds and passions that Emily Brontë depicts in *Wuthering Heights* (1847), a novel as popular today as *Pride and Prejudice*.

VOLUME THREE, CHAPTERS XI AND XII (CHAPTERS 53 AND 54)

SUMMARY

- Lydia and Wickham leave Longbourn for Newcastle and will not return for at least a year.
- Mrs Bennet is disconsolate until she hears that Bingley is to return to Netherfield.
- Mr Bennet refuses to call on Bingley but Bingley and Darcy visit Longbourn. Darcy is silent and less friendly than he was when they met at Pemberley. Jane's beauty seems to be affecting Bingley.
- Bingley and Darcy come to dinner and Bingley chooses to sit next to Jane. Elizabeth sees him looking at Darcy as if asking permission. Darcy and Elizabeth exchange few words.

ANALYSIS

BINGLEY RETURNS TO NETHERFIELD

Mrs Bennet asks her husband to visit Bingley, a repetition of her request with which the events of the novel began. News of his impending arrival 'to shoot there for several weeks' (p. 313) returns the reader to the first page of the novel when 'a young man of large fortune from the north of England' (p. 5) first gets local tongues wagging. Mrs Bennet's spirits are instantly enlivened by the news. Jane on the other hand changes colour and appears 'distressed' (p. 313) though she insists to Elizabeth that her reaction has more to do with her 'dread' of 'other people's remarks' (p. 314) than with any feelings she has for Bingley.

STUDY FOCUS: TRUE FEELINGS   A02

Austen is preoccupied in this chapter with Elizabeth's reactions to seeing Darcy again now that her feelings towards him have changed, although even Jane does not know of her truest feelings. Both Jane and Elizabeth are busy guarding themselves against inappropriate and immodest hopes with regard to Bingley and Darcy.

In this they are contrasted with their mother, who is as unashamed as ever in her matchmaking, though **ironically** she is determined to be rude to Darcy. Her ignorance of the fact that Darcy has saved Lydia from 'irremediable infamy' (p. 317) and of Elizabeth's newly found partiality leads to much embarrassment. Elizabeth is embarrassed by the exaggerated 'civility' (p. 317) that Mrs Bennet shows towards Bingley when they visit Longbourn and her 'cold and ceremonious politeness' (p. 317) to Darcy. Elizabeth is miserable since she feels that the society of Bingley and Darcy cannot bring pleasure or a happy conclusion, only 'wretchedness' (p. 319). She cannot help noticing, however, how 'the beauty of her sister re-kindled the admiration of her former lover' (p. 319). Contrastingly, her irritation with Darcy's reserve is amusing to the reader, who sees it as typical of his behaviour throughout the novel.

GRADE BOOSTER   A02

What are the circumstances that lead to Elizabeth's embarrassment in *Pride and Prejudice*, and what do these episodes tell us about Austen's views of human psychology and behaviour?

GRADE BOOSTER   A02

How does the **narrator** want us to view Darcy's persistent inability to acknowledge his feelings and his concealment of them?

GLOSSARY

318   **covies** broods of partridges

VOLUME THREE, CHAPTER XIII (CHAPTER 55)

SUMMARY

- Bingley and Mr Bennet go shooting. Mr Bennet finds Bingley pleasant company and he is invited to dinner at Longbourn that evening.
- Bingley proposes to Jane and is accepted.
- Jane is overjoyed and goes to tell her mother the good news. Bingley returns and Elizabeth congratulates him. He goes to ask Mr Bennet's permission to marry Jane.
- Jane tells Elizabeth that Bingley did not know that she was in London during the spring and blames his sisters.

ANALYSIS

HAPPINESS

After Bingley leaves the room, Jane confesses to her beloved sister 'with the liveliest emotion' that she is 'the happiest creature in the world' (p. 279). Jane's happiness is shown to be true and deserved, and her expressions of delight can be compared to the hollowness of Mr Collins's much-repeated phrase 'happiest of men' (p. 102) earlier in the novel and perhaps also to Charlotte's rather measured expectations of happiness after accepting Mr Collins's hand in marriage herself: 'I am convinced that my chance of happiness with him is as fair, as most people can boast on entering the marriage state' (p. 123). Elizabeth marvels that after 'all his sister's falsehood and contrivance! the happiest, wisest, most reasonable end' (p. 328) has finally been reached. 'If I could but see *you* as happy!' (p. 331) wishes Jane.

STUDY FOCUS: PUBLIC AND PRIVATE — A02

In this chapter, Elizabeth surprises Jane and Bingley during a private conversation. Austen does not attempt to show how Jane and Bingley talk to each other, preferring the safety of seeing events from Elizabeth's point of view. Similarly we are not provided with Elizabeth's congratulatory speech to Jane. Much of the plan of these final chapters, in which Elizabeth is still in suspense as to Darcy's intentions, is to temper the possible sentimentality of the happy ending for which we are still confidently hoping. Austen wants to show how proper, intelligent, demure young women should behave.

At the end of this chapter, the fickleness of public opinion and sentiment is mocked by Austen: 'The Bennets were speedily pronounced to be the luckiest family in the world, though only a few weeks before … they had been generally proved to be marked out for misfortune' (p. 331). The semi-legal verbs 'pronounced' and 'proved' ironically draw attention to the worthlessness and insubstantiality of public opinion, though at least here the neighbours are taking pleasure in the Bennets' good fortune, rather than, as before, delighting in their downfall.

CHECK THE FILM — A04

In the BBC adaptation, we see Bingley and Darcy talking in private about their situation; Bingley is angry that Darcy did not tell him of Jane Bennet's presence in London, but he still craves his friend's permission to pursue her. In *Pride and Prejudice*, as in all her novels, Austen never depicts conversations between men away from the presence of women.

CHECK THE BOOK — A04

In *Romantics, Rebels and Reactionaries* (1981), Marilyn Butler writes: 'The heroines of her first five novels all marry country clergymen, or a landed gentleman living on his land … The point in each case is that the village community's leader is being sought, the true hereditary gentleman. It is this social concern which is new with Jane Austen, the product of her uneasy times.'

VOLUME THREE, CHAPTERS XIV AND XV (CHAPTERS 56 AND 57)

- Lady Catherine de Bourgh pays a surprise visit to Longbourn.

- She attempts to extort a promise from Elizabeth that she will never accept Darcy. Elizabeth refuses to comply and Lady Catherine leaves, 'most seriously displeased' (p. 339).

- Elizabeth wonders about Lady Catherine's visit. How would Darcy respond to such an attack? Supposing that her ladyship is highly thought of by her nephew, she imagines that Darcy will never come to see her again.

- Mr Collins writes to Mr Bennet to convey Lady Catherine's opposition to the match. He also expresses his shock that Lydia and Wickham have been allowed to visit Longbourn. Mr Bennet shares with Elizabeth his amusement at the letter.

ANALYSIS

ELIZABETH AND LADY CATHERINE

Though Jane Austen is shy of presenting lovers dramatically, she has no such timidity when presenting Lady Catherine's outraged snobbery in full flood. Elizabeth's confident rebuttal of all Lady Catherine's insults and demands is almost thrilling. When Lady Catherine states that she is 'entitled' to know all Darcy's 'dearest concerns', Elizabeth assertively replies, 'But you are not entitled to know *mine*, nor will such behaviour as this, ever induce me to be explicit' (p. 335). Here are pride and prejudice in all their irrational fury, and they fail to prevail against a young woman's good sense. **Ironically**, Lady Catherine's efforts speed the union of Darcy and Elizabeth, exactly the opposite of her intention (see Chapter XVI (Chapter 58)).

STUDY FOCUS: FATHER AND DAUGHTER

Mr Bennet, unaware of Elizabeth's sentiments towards Darcy, finds the letter from Mr Collins ridiculous – particularly since it names Darcy as Elizabeth's suitor: 'but *his* perfect indifference, and *your* pointed dislike, make it so delightfully absurd!' (p. 344) exclaims an amused Mr Bennet. Elizabeth is forced to laugh at her father's jokes, when she would rather cry. The necessity of Elizabeth concealing her feelings is depicted as painful for her, but such misunderstandings are typical of comic situations, and the reader is still sure that the book is essentially comic in nature.

The scene serves also to point out Mr Bennet's lack of insight and show how his ironic vision insulates him from a sympathetic and lively interest in those around him. Lizzy is his favourite daughter, and yet he has not noticed anything about her emotional state. The capacity to penetrate the surface of events, and understand the realities of proper feeling and morality behind it, is a highly prized attribute in Jane Austen's created world. Of course, the **narrator** has more 'penetration' (p. 342) than any of the characters, since she knows how things are going to end.

VOLUME THREE, CHAPTER XVI (CHAPTER 58)

SUMMARY

- Elizabeth finds herself alone with Darcy.
- She explains that her feelings have changed towards him.
- Darcy proposes to Elizabeth for a second time and is accepted by her.
- They discuss their relationship at some length.

ANALYSIS

DARCY'S VISIT

In this chapter, Elizabeth discovers that she has Lady Catherine to thank for Darcy's visit. Darcy tells Elizabeth that she was right to refuse him at his first proposal. He acknowledges that he was spoiled as a child and almost encouraged to be 'selfish and overbearing' (p. 349). Elizabeth mentions his altered behaviour at Pemberley and he tells her that his aim was to convince her that he was sufficiently generous to forget the past.

Elizabeth discovers that before Darcy left for London he told Bingley that Jane was not indifferent to him. Bingley was angry when he found out that his friend had prevented him from seeing Jane while she was in London, but his anger soon passed when Jane returned his affections.

STUDY FOCUS: AN INTIMATE CONVERSATION · A02

It is Elizabeth who initiates the serious and intimate conversation that occupies this chapter. Both of them explain the true state of their feelings with regard to the other at every stage in the haphazard development of their relationship. They both have a lot to make up for, as this is the first time they have talked alone since Darcy's refused proposal. Not only does Elizabeth instigate the conversation, but she shows her control at the end by holding back from teasing Darcy.

Before the deserved 'happiness' can be fully allowed, they must map out the rights and wrongs of how they have behaved and arrive at a true understanding of what was and was not appropriate. It was Elizabeth's reproof of Darcy's failure to behave in a 'more gentleman-like manner' (p. 347) that stung him into rethinking his mode of behaviour. Manners here stand not merely for polish, but for the essence of the way sensitive and intelligent human beings should behave towards each other.

At the moment when Elizabeth and Darcy are most involved in confessing their love for each other, the narrator shies away from putting into words what passes between them. Is Austen incapable of imagining this crucial passage of feeling when Darcy renews his proposal? Or does she heighten her readers' engagement by leaving such a moment to their imaginations?

CHECK THE BOOK · A04

How gentlemen should behave is a constant preoccupation of eighteenth- and nineteenth-century writing, and is a central interest of *Pride and Prejudice*. Robin Gilmour's *The Idea of the Gentleman in the Victorian Novel* (1981) is a general study of the theme.

CONTEXT · A04

Note how a good marriage is assumed to be the only possible happy conclusion to a young woman's hopes and intentions at that time; Charlotte Lucas states that it is the 'only provision' for women in her position (p. 120).

VOLUME THREE, CHAPTER XVII (CHAPTER 59)

SUMMARY

- Elizabeth confesses all to an astonished Jane.
- The next day Mr Bennet gives his consent, and Mrs Bennet has to revise her opinion of Darcy.

ANALYSIS

REVELATIONS

This is a chapter of high comedy, in which Elizabeth has to face the consequence of disguising her true feelings for so long. First Jane has to be convinced, then her father, then her mother. Each responds in their own way. Jane wants Elizabeth to be more serious. Mr Bennet is admirable in his real concern that Lizzy should only marry someone that she truly respects. We should see this as a comment on his own marriage, as well as a proper understanding of Elizabeth. He is less admirable in his complacent pleasure in the fact that he will not have to pay Darcy back for Lydia's rescue.

KEY QUOTATION: VOLUME THREE, CHAPTER XVII (CHAPTER 59) A01

Key quotation: 'Oh my sweetest Lizzy! how rich and how great you will be! What pin-money, what jewels, what carriages you will have! Jane's is nothing to it – nothing at all. I am so pleased – so happy. Such a charming man!' (pp. 357–8)

- Mrs Bennet is quickly won over by a moment's thought about Darcy's wealth. She is soon dwelling on how rich Elizabeth will become, and how handsome and charming the 'disagreeable Mr Darcy' has suddenly turned out to be.

- There is a breathless and haphazard quality to the phrases that tumble from Mrs Bennet's mouth achieved by the short sentences and phrases, the many exclamations and the use of dashes. See Volume One, Chapter V (Chapter 5) for another good example of Mrs Bennet's **style** of speaking.

- Much of the comedy here comes from the swiftness with which Mrs Bennet assumes new opinions and sentiments; instant comparisons are drawn with Jane's match, and Darcy's virtues are extolled with as much fervour as she once denounced his vices.

GRADE BOOSTER A02

What does this chapter add to your understanding of Austen's attitude to money in relation to love and marriage in *Pride and Prejudice*?

CRITICAL VIEWPOINT A02

In 1866 a reviewer wrote of *Pride and Prejudice*: 'In construction the book is nearly perfect; the principal theme – the victory over D'Arcy's pride and Elizabeth's prejudice – sprouts at the beginning, flowers in the middle, and, without forcing, bears fine fruit at the end.'

GLOSSARY

357 **pin-money** a wife's spending money

VOLUME THREE, CHAPTER XVIII (CHAPTER 60)

SUMMARY

- Letters are exchanged about Elizabeth and Darcy's wedding.
- The Collinses arrive at Lucas Lodge, anxious to avoid the storm of Lady Catherine's displeasure.
- Elizabeth looks forward to being at Pemberley.

ANALYSIS

EARLIEST FEELINGS

Elizabeth questions Darcy about how and when he fell in love with her. She asks him whether she admired her for her 'impertinence' (p. 359) and he agrees, though he prefers to call it 'the liveliness of your mind' (p. 359). The two lovers quibble happily about their past behaviour. Elizabeth is playful and teasing ('To be sure, you knew no actual good of me', p. 359), Darcy more formal and serious ('Was there no good in your affectionate behaviour to Jane?', p. 360). So accustomed is Darcy to have the admiration of women like Miss Bingley that Elizabeth's freedom of spirit in teasing him makes her especially attractive.

LETTERS

Austen provides the text of Elizabeth's gleeful letter to her aunt in which she 'thanks her for not going to the Lakes' (p. 361). We are not shown what Darcy writes to Lady Catherine. Mr Bennet's letter to Mr Collins is wholly lacking in the **ironic** politeness that is usually his mode of dealing with the pompous clergyman. In recommending that Mr Collins court Darcy rather than his aunt, it cuts right through the hypocrisy of Mr Collins's need to curry favour with the rich and powerful in order to secure his advancement in the church.

STUDY FOCUS: THE IN-LAWS **A02**

Dealing honestly with money is an occasionally surprising but consistent aspect of the narrative. Austen is equally unsentimental in portraying the difficulties that confront Elizabeth with regard to her relatives' lack of good manners and sophistication. Darcy must be prevented whenever possible from having to deal with Mrs Bennet and Mrs Philips. In *Pride and Prejudice* as in Austen's other novels, intelligent and witty characters illustrate by their forbearance and courtesy the proper way of dealing with bores and those without taste. Darcy's duty is to be unfailingly polite. However, in the next chapter we see that even someone so unfailingly good-natured as Bingley moves away from the neighbourhood of his in-laws as soon as is decently possible.

VOLUME THREE, CHAPTER XIX (CHAPTER 61)

SUMMARY

- Some time has passed. Both Jane and Elizabeth are happily married.
- The narrator updates the reader about the circumstances of many characters and about their visits to Pemberley to spend time with the happy couple.

ANALYSIS

THE BENNETS

We learn that Mrs Bennet is happy but no less silly than ever. Mr Bennet misses Elizabeth and often pays surprise visits to Pemberley. While their parents appear little changed, we are told that Kitty has improved thanks to the time that she spends with her older sisters: 'removed from the influence of Lydia's example, she became, by proper attention and management, less irritable, less ignorant, and less insipid' (p. 365). Mary is the only daughter still at home, working on her 'accomplishments' (p. 365) and keeping her mother company. After a year at Netherfield the Bingleys move to within thirty miles of Pemberley, to both Jane's and Elizabeth's great delight.

Lydia and Wickham live a life that is 'unsettled in the extreme' (p. 366), overspending their income and moving continually. Elizabeth often sends Lydia money that she has saved from her own expenses and Lydia is even allowed to visit Pemberley when Darcy is away. We are shown Lydia's letter to Elizabeth: it is astonishingly crude and bold in its egocentric application for help and money.

OTHER KEY CHARACTERS

Miss Bingley, 'mortified' by Darcy's marriage, manages to deal politely with Elizabeth so as to retain the right of visiting at Pemberley. Georgiana Darcy and Elizabeth are very close, although Georgiana is often alarmed by Elizabeth's 'lively, sportive' (p. 366) way of treating Darcy. The reader is pleased to hear that Elizabeth's spirit is in no way dampened by marriage. We learn that even the implacable Lady Catherine is prevailed upon to forgive the couple, and visits Pemberley, propelled chiefly by her curiosity to see how Elizabeth is coping.

STUDY FOCUS: NARRATIVE CLOSURE | A02

In this final chapter the narrator closes up the loose ends of the narrative with a 'happily ever after' explanation of all that awaits the characters. Any easy fairy-tale sentiment is kept well at bay by the clipped, detached and **ironic** mode of description in which she sums up events. Mr Bennet delights in going to Pemberley, 'especially when he was least expected' (p. 364). Mary, it is suggested, relaxes into moralising 'over every morning visit' (p. 365), once her two more attractive sisters are no longer rivals.

The novel ends, however, on a more tender note: Darcy's affection for the Gardiners, and the couple's gratitude towards them for bringing Elizabeth to Derbyshire so as to be 'the means of uniting them' (p. 367).

CHECK THE FILM | A04

The BBC version ends sentimentally with the double wedding of Elizabeth and Jane, an event that is quite missing from the novel. Austen as **narrator** ties up all the loose ends and the fates of the minor characters at the end of her text.

CHECK THE BOOK | A03

Couples who arrive at love through teasing and disputation are a stereotype of comic writing, as for example in Shakespeare's *Much Ado about Nothing*, in which Beatrice and Benedick bicker and quarrel before falling in love.

GLOSSARY

366 **restoration of peace** after the Napoleonic Wars

CHARACTERS

CHARACTERISATION

Jane Austen seems to enjoy discussing her characters, recounting their conversations with each other through her ironic narration, and showing how they behave both in times of leisure and in times of stress. For further discussion of the **narrator** see **Structure, form and language**. Self-sufficient though they may seem, the characters are essentially part of the novelist's plan for discussing a number of ideas through the narration of a series of events. When writing about the novel, it is necessary to keep a sharp sense of the roles these fictitious characters are playing within the author's overall plan and vision.

CHECK THE BOOK A03

A short essay, 'Characterization in Jane Austen' by John Bayley, is included in *The Jane Austen Handbook* edited by J. David Grey (1986). A famous general study of novel-writing, which pays attention to character, is E. M. Forster's *Aspects of the Novel* (1927).

PHYSICALITY AND MORALITY

One striking aspect of Austen's writing is the lack of physical descriptions of characters. Where Austen does indulge in more specific and individualised comment about a character's appearance, it is usually in direct connection with that character's place in the action or the moral framework of the story. For example, we are told in Volume One, Chapter II (Chapter 2), that Lydia, though the youngest, is the tallest of the five sisters. These comments must be seen in relation to her behaviour: at sixteen she is physically a woman, but emotionally immature and out of control.

When Austen gives the reader a physical detail about a character, it would seem that her reasons for doing so go beyond an interest in describing appearance for its own sake. Darcy is captivated by 'a pair of fine eyes in the face of a pretty woman' (p. 27). When 'with great intrepidity' he admits these are Elizabeth's (p. 28), his comment is remorselessly used against him by Miss Bingley (who had expected a compliment to herself). Elizabeth's beautiful eyes – we are told they are 'dark' (p. 24) – therefore serve a larger purpose than simple description. They allow Darcy to stand up for her and for himself, and then they serve Caroline Bingley with an opportunity for malice.

What finally interests the narrator is not her characters' appearance, but their moral qualities, or lack of them. It is through their attitudes to these qualities that the differences between characters are revealed. In their behaviour and reactions, characters show their discrimination and their capacity for good taste and judgement.

ELIZABETH BENNET

WHO IS ELIZABETH?

- Elizabeth is the second oldest of the Bennet sisters.
- She is is Mr Bennet's favourite daughter and she is also very close to her sister Jane, her aunt Mrs Gardiner and her friend Charlotte Lucas.
- We frequently view events from her perspective.
- She is the novel's heroine in the sense that she is the main focus of the reader's interest, though she makes mistakes and is not particularly heroic.
- In the novel's concern with pride and with prejudice, she and Darcy are the main players. Their path to a better understanding of each other and ultimately falling in love is the novel's central plot.
- By the end of the novel she is Darcy's wife and the mistress of Pemberley.

WIT AND HUMOUR

Elizabeth Bennet is intelligent and lively, and her 'quickness' (p. 7) of mind is made evident in her taste for witty and teasing conversation, where she likes to adopt striking and independent views. Evidence for this is best found in her conversations with Bingley, his sisters and Darcy when she is looking after Jane at Netherfield in Volume One, Chapters VIII, IX and XI (Chapters 8, 9 and 11).

She likes to laugh at people, including herself. We are told after Darcy refused to dance with her that 'She told the story with great spirit amongst her friends; for she had a lively, playful disposition, which delighted in anything ridiculous' (p. 14). It is this quality of humour that attracts Darcy. Her rival Miss Bingley calls it 'that little something, bordering on conceit and impertinence' (p. 51), but the **narrator** has already told us that 'there was a mixture of sweetness and archness in her manner which made it difficult for her to affront anybody' (p. 51).

IRONY

Elizabeth shares her capacity for **irony** with her father, and with the narrator. This allows her to stand away from situations and offer judgements on them, sometimes (though not as often as the narrator or her father) in the form of saying the opposite of what she really means. 'Mr Darcy is all politeness', she remarks in Volume One, Chapter VI (Chapter 6) (p. 27), as a way of avoiding dancing with him: we can guess that she is remembering his rudeness to her.

STUDY FOCUS: REFLECTION AND REALISATION A02

As the novel progresses we start to share more of Elizabeth's thoughts and see her more inwardly, often by means of the technique called **free indirect discourse** or thought, where we are presented with thoughts in the manner of indirect speech. A key passage in reviewing Elizabeth's growth is Volume Two, Chapter XIII (Chapter 36), when we see her painfully coming to terms with her mistaken understanding of Wickham and Darcy while reading Darcy's letter: 'She grew absolutely ashamed of herself' (p. 201). She has to take in information that  contradicts some of her prejudiced judgements, and in doing so realises that she has not been as sharp a reader of character as she has confidently supposed. She blames herself for not having recognised the smack of 'impropriety' (p. 200) in Wickham's behaviour, and allowing herself to be deceived by his charm.

KEY QUOTATIONS: ELIZABETH A01

Key quotation 1:

'Elizabeth continued her walk alone … springing over puddles with impatient activity, and finding herself at last within view of the house, with weary ancles, dirty stockings, and a face glowing with the warmth of exercise.' (p. 33)

- She is active and robust, to the point of being considered unfeminine by her enemies. Her dirty petticoat is shocking to Miss Bingley and a subject of ridicule.
- Darcy and Bingley, however, find the results of her vigour appealing and attractive.
- The haste with which Elizabeth walks to Netherfield and her lack of attention to her appearance also show us how concerned she is about her sister's welfare and her determination to see her.

Key quotation 2:

'It has been coming on so gradually, that I hardly know when it began. But I believe I must date it from my first seeing his beautiful grounds at Pemberley.' (p. 353)

- Elizabeth is revealing to her sister Jane that she has fallen in love with Darcy and agreed to marry him.
- Is Elizabeth entirely joking when she remarks that she fell in love with Darcy when she saw Pemberley? Is one of the lessons that Elizabeth has to learn to place true value on Darcy's wealth and position, the very source of his pride?
- Earlier in the novel, Elizabeth feels with some indignation that Charlotte Lucas has sacrificed 'every better feeling to worldly advantage' (p. 123) by agreeing to marry Mr Collins but Elizabeth acknowledges here, however teasingly, that 'worldly advantage' has been gained by herself too, only with a more sympathetic husband.

CRITICAL VIEWPOINT A03

Only Darcy and Elizabeth develop as characters in *Pride and Prejudice*. Perhaps it is because of their superior intelligence that they are marked out by the narrator as capable of moral evolution in a way that their friends, neighbours and relatives are not. Or it may just be an aspect of novelistic convention to concentrate only on the 'juvenile leads', as they would be called in the theatre: the paired young **protagonist** and **antagonist** around whom the story revolves.

JANE BENNET

WHO IS JANE?

- Jane is the eldest of the Bennet sisters. She is the most sweet tempered and by general agreement the most beautiful. Bingley, after two dances with her at the first assembly, says that she is the 'most beautiful creature I ever beheld' (p. 13).

- We are not given any specific details about Jane's appearance except that she is heavier than Elizabeth and cannot run as fast as her (Volume Three, Chapter VII (Chapter 49)).

- She is optimistic, patient and constant in her affections, as her long wait for Bingley shows.

CANDOUR

The **narrator** writes of Jane's 'mild and steady candour' (p. 136). Jane is candid in the old meaning of the word: she looks at the world without bias or malice. Candour is the opposite of prejudice. Jane is, for example, a lone voice prepared to think the best of Darcy in Volume One, Chapter V (Chapter 5): 'he never speaks much unless among his intimate acquaintance. With *them* he is remarkably agreeable' (p. 20). The reader can map the development of Elizabeth's character change alongside Jane's steady views and temperament.

CHECK THE FILM A04

Compare the casting and performances of the actresses who play Elizabeth, Jane and the other sisters in film and TV adaptations of the novel.

STUDY FOCUS: FRIENDSHIP A02

Sisters Jane and Elizabeth are close friends and confidantes. At several points in the novel, their intimate communications to each other are how the reader learns of an important development in the plot such as Lydia and Wickham's elopement in Volume Three, Chapter IV (Chapter 46), or of a changed attitude or feeling such as when Jane reluctantly concludes that Caroline Bingley has not had her interests at heart as a true friend would: 'we shall be on good terms again; though we can never be what we once were to each other' (p. 330). By contrast, in Volume Three, Chapter XVII (Chapter 59), we are told that Elizabeth 'opened her heart to Jane' (p. 352) and of 'half the night spent in conversation' (p. 354), indicative of a true bond, not the semblance of friendship that Caroline showed Jane.

KEY QUOTATION: JANE A01

Key quotation:

'"My dear Jane!" exclaimed Elizabeth, "you are too good ... I feel as if I had never done you justice, or loved you as you deserve."

'Miss Bennet eagerly disclaimed all extraordinary merit, and threw back the praise on her sister's warm affection.' (p. 132)

- Jane is shown here in difficult circumstances but is typically sweet-natured, modest and generous in her views of others.

- On the question of 'whether Bingley's regard had really died away' (p. 132), Jane stoically accepts that hope is over. She says she has 'nothing to reproach him with' (p. 132).

- Elizabeth's views on Bingley's feelings are different to her sister's but she believes in and affirms her sister's sincerity and goodness. Jane's essential, almost stereotypical goodness makes her a perfect contrast to the more difficult Elizabeth.

LYDIA BENNET

WHO IS LYDIA?

- Lydia is the youngest of the Bennet sisters and is her mother's favourite daughter.
- She shares with her mother a partiality for men in uniform and an obsession with fashionable clothes.
- Her elopement with Wickham is a shocking development and perhaps the most dramatic episode in the novel. Their eventual marriage is brought about by Darcy's influence.

FLIRTATIOUS

Lydia is brazenly flirtatious and vain. This is clearly shown from the moment that word spreads of the militia's arrival in Meryton in Volume One, Chapter VII (Chapter 7). In the world of Austen's novels, irresponsibility over small things like lunch money (see Volume Two, Chapter XVI (Chapter 39)) can presage future disasters on a larger scale. Lydia lacks all understanding – or does not care – about the moral and social consequences of running away with Wickham. Her unworried expectation that living with him would probably lead to marriage at some time or other is profoundly shocking to Jane and Elizabeth, and indeed to their father.

STUDY FOCUS: SEX AND MARRIAGE   A02

From a modern perspective, we might choose to see something positive in Lydia's self-confidence and spiritedness, some modern 'girl power' certainly lacking in, say, Jane. Marriage for Lydia is no more than an opportunity for 'very good fun' (p. 299) but it is clear from the reactions of most of her relatives that her behaviour is likely to be viewed as shameful by the wider world. Her disappearance causes a family furore, but **ironically** it is the means by which Darcy and Elizabeth will be reconciled. Darcy's innocent sister Georgiana was also prey to Wickham's charms, allowing Darcy to sympathise with the Bennet predicament, and even to feel himself somewhat to blame. However, the novel ultimately shows Lydia to be responsible for her own actions and the reader is likely to share Elizabeth's view that her sister has been 'thoughtless' (p. 265) and has brought 'humiliation' and 'misery' (p. 264) upon her family.

KEY QUOTATION: LYDIA   A01

Key quotation:

'She had high animal spirits, and a sort of natural self-consequence, which the attentions of the officers, to whom her uncle's good dinners and her own easy manners recommended her, had increased into assurance.' (p. 45)

- Lydia is the tallest sister and fully developed physically at fifteen.
- 'Animal', 'easy', and 'assurance' are all danger signals in one so young. Does 'animal' hint at her sexuality?

> **GRADE BOOSTER**   A02
>
> Look back at passages of Lydia's extended speech, for example in Volume Two, Chapter XVI and Volume Three, Chapter IX (Chapter 39 and Chapter 51). How does Austen use these passages to convey Lydia's outspoken and unreflective personality?

MARY BENNET

WHO IS MARY?

- Mary is the middle sister in the Bennet family.
- She is self-important, pious, moralistic and pedantic.
- Mary likes to read and plays the piano well, but without feeling, and for much longer than anyone wants to listen.

MARY ON 'PRIDE'

At the end of Volume One, Chapter V (Chapter 5), Mary delivers a dreary little monologue on pride. As it deals with one of the book's explicit **themes**, it is not without interest as a textbook statement of the difference between pride and vanity, and it shows that Austen can use Mary as a mouthpiece for a point of view: a serious distinction is here concealed in comic pomposity. However, Mary is generally ignored, though her father sometimes enjoys teasing her.

STUDY FOCUS: MARY'S FUTURE | A02

At the end of the story, the **narrator** hints at tensions that lie behind her role in the family: 'Mary was obliged to mix more with the world … and as she was no longer mortified by comparisons between her sisters' beauty and her own, it was suspected by her father that she submitted to the change without much reluctance' (p. 365). This is the only example of her development as a character, and indeed so constant is her minor role in the **plot** that she is something of a **caricature**.

CHECK THE BOOK | A03

Austen's *Mansfield Park* (1814) is a study of a pious and passively 'good' character, Fanny Price, who has none of the buoyant spirit of, for example, Elizabeth Bennet. Mary's piety, however, is not combined with sympathy or kindness: her ready agreement with Mr Collins's condemnation of Lydia is typical of her.

KEY QUOTATION: MARY | A01

Key quotation:

Commenting on Mr Collins's letter, Mary says:

'"In point of composition … his letter does not seem defective. The idea of the olive branch perhaps is not wholly new, yet I think it is well expressed."' (p. 63)

- Like her father, Mary takes refuge in books, but she has not learnt ironic detachment as the juxtaposition of Mr Bennet's opinions on Mr Collins's letter with her own shows.
- Mary tends to talk in a rather impersonal way, relying on received wisdom rather than her own insights.
- There is humour in the notion that Mary, whose manner of expressing herself is, as we have seen, rather verbose and boring, should be impressed by the equally tiresome and clichéd stylings of Mr Collins.

KITTY (CATHERINE) BENNET

WHO IS KITTY?

- Catherine or Kitty is the second youngest Bennet sister.
- Kitty plays little part in the novel except as a parallel and contrast to Lydia.

LYDIA'S INFLUENCE ON KITTY

Kitty joins Lydia in the enthusiastic pursuit of officers until Lydia's removal to Brighton. She is being led astray by Lydia until the better influences of her older sisters take over, so successfully that she becomes 'less ignorant, less irritable, and less insipid' (p. 364–5).

MR BENNET

WHO IS MR BENNET?

- Mr Bennet is the father of Jane, Elizabeth and the other Bennet girls and is the current incumbent of Longbourn.
- He is bookish, clever and humorous in his **ironic** mockery of his wife and daughters.
- The gulf in understanding between him and his wife is huge.
- Over the course of the novel, we see him as morally indolent and self-indulgent, despite his attractions as a character.

FLAWS AND FAILURES

Mr Bennet represents the dangers of an ironic disposition when it is unmixed with moral and social probity, virtues possessed by his fellow ironists Elizabeth and the narrator. His failure to follow Elizabeth's advice not to allow Lydia to go to Brighton (Volume Two, Chapter XVIII (Chapter 41)) is the clearest example of his misjudgement; at least he has the grace to admit this and apologise (Volume Three, Chapter VI (Chapter 48)). Though he fails to live up to his responsibilities as father and head of the family, he remains the source of pleasant jokes right up to the end of the novel: 'I admire all my three sons-in-law highly … Wickham, perhaps, is my favourite' (p. 358).

CHECK THE BOOK A03

Is a tendency to be ironic always tied to mockery? For an example of irony unusually combined with compassion, read Dr Johnson's short life of his friend Richard Savage, in *Lives of the English Poets* (1781).

STUDY FOCUS: FACING UP TO PROBLEMS — A02

The issue of the entail of Longbourn hangs over Mr Bennet and his family, but he has put off doing anything about it, preferring to hope for many years for the birth of a son that would put things to rights (Volume Three, Chapter VIII (Chapter 50)). His casual acceptance of the financial resolution of Lydia's marriage shows how inactive he can be. Mr Bennet's pleasure at not having to do anything seems too easy and superficial a response. We cannot admire his indolence, his fecklessness or his uselessness in the face of the grave situation in which the family finds itself. Mr Gardiner and Darcy take over tracing and dealing with Wickham and Lydia. At this point in the novel his humour deserts him, but not for long (Volume Three, Chapter VI (Chapter 48)); but would he be more likeable if he sank into depressive gloom? We could agree that he has at least found a way of dealing cheerfully with an unhappy marriage and five daughters.

KEY QUOTATION: MR BENNET — A01

Key quotation: 'Her father, captivated by youth and beauty, and that appearance of good humour, which youth and beauty generally give, had married a woman whose weak understanding and illiberal mind, had very early in their marriage put an end to all real affection for her.' (p. 228)

- The narrator explains that Mr Bennet married his wife for her 'youth and beauty' but that he no longer has 'real affection for her'.
- Their marriage represents a warning about taking such an irrational and impetuous approach to domestic happiness.
- Understanding and respect are presented as sounder foundations for marriage than merely youth, beauty and the appearance of good humour.

MRS BENNET

WHO IS MRS BENNET?

- Mrs Bennet, her husband and their five daughters live at Longbourn.
- From the very beginning of the novel, we know of Mrs Bennet's quest to marry her daughters, a quest that instigates the novel's entire **plot**.
- Mrs Bennet is portrayed as superficial in her understanding, trivial in her interests and mistaken in her judgements throughout the whole novel.

COMEDY

Whereas we can laugh with Mr Bennet, we laugh *at* Mrs Bennet. Our view of her begins to be formed by the narrator's acidic summary very early in the text: 'She was a woman of mean understanding, little information, and uncertain temper' (p. 7). Her behaviour and language are often openly comical and enjoyable to read, but sometimes it is almost sad that she is so incapable of responding to situations with more good sense and less nagging and hysterical silliness. In so far as **caricatures** present a view of unchangeable human character, their clowning often has this distressing aspect.

GRADE BOOSTER A02

Look up 'propriety' in a dictionary, and then trace how and when the word is used in *Pride and Prejudice*. Try searching one of the online texts of the novel, which can be found on the main sites devoted to Austen.

STUDY FOCUS: MANNERS   A02

It transpires over the course of the novel that Mrs Bennet's often vulgar behaviour is an obstacle to Darcy's developing interest in Elizabeth and his reason for persuading Bingley to leave Meryton and ignore Jane. It is not the position of the Bennet family, but their manners that shock Darcy. He characterises their behaviour at the Netherfield ball in his letter to Elizabeth: 'The situation of your mother's family, though objectionable, was as nothing in comparison of that total want of propriety so frequently, so almost uniformly betrayed by herself, by your three younger sisters, and occasionally even by your father' (p. 193). The language may be different but the situation is familiar today: a young person is cruelly embarrassed by the behaviour of her parents in a public place. Later on, in her pleasure at Lydia's marriage with Wickham, Mrs Bennet shows a more alarming blindness to financial and moral propriety.

KEY QUOTATION: MRS BENNET   A01

Key quotation: 'Nothing could console and nothing could appease her.—Nor did that day wear out her resentment. A week elapsed before she could see Elizabeth without scolding her, a month passed away before she could speak to Sir William or Lady Lucas without being rude, and many months were gone before she could at all forgive their daughter.' (p. 125)

- After Sir William Lucas has announced Charlotte's engagement, Mrs Bennet's reaction demonstrates her inability to disguise her self-pity, malice and naked rivalry with her neighbours.
- Mrs Bennet shows a characteristic inability to argue rationally and instead simply gives way to her feelings. This leads her very often to contradict herself and to switch from one subject to another in a muddled way.

MR DARCY

WHO IS MR DARCY?

- Darcy is a wealthy gentleman whose home is Pemberley in Derbyshire.
- He has a younger sister, Georgiana.
- Darcy is proud, and he is prejudiced. We may dislike him for this – just as Elizabeth does – but we are also asked to consider whether sometimes such feelings may be appropriate.
- We are told that 'Darcy was clever. He was at the same time haughty, reserved, and fastidious, and his manners, though well bred, were not inviting … Darcy was continually giving offence' (p. 18).
- He overcomes his pride to marry the woman he loves, Elizabeth, at the end of the novel.

FIRST IMPRESSIONS

Darcy is in many respects an unattractive character at the start of the novel. Austen seems to enjoy creating difficult characters, but Darcy is difficult to accept in a manner quite different from her caricatures. In Volume I, Chapter XI (Chapter 11), Elizabeth manages to confront him with some of his potential failings, in witty discussion of the fact that 'Mr Darcy is not to be laughed at!' (p. 56). She concludes that he is implacably resentful and hates everybody. (See **Extended commentary: Volume One.**)

Though honest and capable of self-criticism, Darcy can and does give offence by his behaviour. At his first meeting with Meryton society, when he will dance only with Bingley's sisters, and when he generally disparages the company, he slights Elizabeth in her hearing in a manner parallel with Mrs Bennet's insult to him at the Netherfield Park ball. There may be an element of shyness in his reserve and haughty disdain, but that is perhaps a contemporary way of looking at such behaviour. The narrator does not portray Darcy as shy, and shyness is not an ideal quality in a gentleman who should be equal to all the occasions in which he finds himself. Darcy is poor at dealing with other people, and with his own feelings.

STUDY FOCUS: DARCY'S FIRST PROPOSAL `A02`

Darcy's proposal to Elizabeth in Volume Two, Chapter XI (Chapter 34) is wrong in strategy and very tactlessly expressed: 'Could you expect me to rejoice in the inferiority of your connections?' (p. 188). Elizabeth's final insulting refusal is spoken with the exaggerations of rage, but it is not unfair. As readers we witness what truth there is in Elizabeth's view of Darcy's manners towards herself and her family; insofar as the narrator has often taken her side, we feel some pleasure in her outburst. She is wrongly angry at Darcy's treatment of Wickham, but rightly angry at his removal of Bingley from Jane's company. He was wrong about Jane's feelings, and in this he lacked penetration, that ability to see what lies behind situations.

In his intricacy of character, proud Darcy has much to learn before the novel can arrive at the satisfactory conclusion of his marriage to Elizabeth. But as his careful, dignified and secretive pursuit of Elizabeth after her angry refusal of his proposal shows, Darcy is more capable of change than any other character in the novel, Elizabeth included.

GRADE BOOSTER `A02`

Volume One, Chapters VII to XII (Chapters 7 to 12), when Elizabeth stays at Netherfield Park, are worth rereading with care in the light of what happens later in the novel, as they lay the foundation for many of the book's **themes**, such as the nature of character, friendship and pride.

CHECK THE FILM   A04

The BBC adaptation makes the differences in character between Darcy and Bingley very clear. Neither the book nor the TV version explains how they should come to be such close friends.

KEY QUOTATION: DARCY   A01

Key quotation: 'I have been a selfish being all my life, in practice, though not in principle. As a child I was taught what was *right*, but I was not taught to correct my temper. I was given good principles, but left to follow them in pride and conceit … Such I was, from eight to eight and twenty; and such I might still have been but for you, dearest, loveliest Elizabeth! What do I not owe you! You taught me a lesson, hard indeed at first, but most advantageous.' (p. 349)

● Darcy's tone in this intimate conversation with Elizabeth is at times pained, honest and self-critical, in a similar vein to his letter in Volume Two, Chapter XII (Chapter 35).

● No other character is shown to be capable of such penetrating self-analysis.

● Darcy is drawn to Bingley by the contrast in their personalities, and this also seems to be the attraction that Elizabeth presents – she can supply a cheerfulness and good nature that he knows himself to lack.

MR BINGLEY

WHO IS MR BINGLEY?

● Bingley is the 'single man in possession of a good fortune' (p. 5) whose arrival at Netherfield as its new tenant sets the novel in motion.

● He is kind, easy-going and attracted by beautiful young women with whom he enjoys dancing. Compared to his friend Darcy, he is somewhat unreflective.

● He is influenced by Darcy and his jealous sister, Caroline, to give up his courtship of Jane Bennet. When Darcy withdraws his disapproval, Bingley and Jane marry at the end of the novel

DOCILITY

Early in the novel, we learn that Darcy admires his friend's 'easiness, openness, ductility of … temper' (p. 18). The most striking example of Bingley's 'ductility' (his docility, or even gullibility) is the way he allows Darcy to persuade him to leave Netherfield. In the book's resolution he is equally ductile, falling easily back in love with Jane, now that he enjoys the approval of this friend: 'it was decided. He placed himself by her' (p. 321). He is the perfect mate for Jane; they share the same sunny optimism with regard to human behaviour. Being less intricate as characters, neither Bingley nor Jane develops over the course of the novel, in contrast with the other pair at the centre of the book's interests, Elizabeth and Darcy.

MR WICKHAM

WHO IS MR WICKHAM?

- Wickham's father was steward of the late Mr Darcy's estate and it was Darcy's father's intention that he should enter the church.
- Wickham claims that Darcy deprived him of his 'living' when in fact he rejected it and tried to elope with Darcy's sister.
- At first, Wickham's handsome appearance and charming conversation catch 'the attention of every lady' (p. 71), including Elizabeth.
- He elopes with Lydia Bennet, paying no heed to the consequences of such a 'disgraceful situation' (p. 305) for Lydia and her family.

WICKHAM'S PAST

The revelations about Wickham's past wrongs that Darcy reveals in his letter to Elizabeth show Wickham to be severely 'in want of principle' (p. 194). Despite the Darcys' financial support for his education and intended career in the church, Wickham repays the family by abandoning this career, behaving wantonly and attempting to elope with Georgiana Darcy. Elizabeth and Jane choose not to share these unfortunate truths more widely, holding out some hope that his morals may be reformed, but the shocking news of his elopement with their youngest sister puts an end to any such hopes.

THE ELOPEMENT

While Lydia is portrayed as wholly infatuated – 'she was sure that they would be married some time or other, and it did not much signify when' – as far as Wickham is concerned, marriage 'had never been *his* design' (p. 305). He has no plan for the future, except to marry money – and Lydia does not have enough of this to make her an interesting partner. The narrator does not spell the matter out, but we must assume that Wickham's interest in Lydia is sexual – she is otherwise of no use to him. It is only because of the financial arrangement, in which Darcy himself secretly plays the key role, that a marriage can be hastily organised and further dishonour avoided.

STUDY FOCUS: APPEARANCE AND REALITY **A02**

In Volume One, Chapter XVI (Chapter 16), Elizabeth had led Wickham on to incriminate the 'abominable' (p. 79) Darcy. In Volume One, Chapter XVII (Chapter 17), Jane wisely remarks that they do not know enough about either man to be sure what is the truth of the matter, but Elizabeth ascribes this simply to Jane's sunny disposition. Caroline Bingley, whom Elizabeth heartily dislikes, warns her quite accurately against Wickham, but Elizabeth puts this down to jealousy and spite (Volume One, Chapter XVIII (Chapter 18)). Prejudice has blinded her and skewed her judgement.

When Wickham much later meets Elizabeth as his sister-in-law, we are shown how he still sets about to charm her, in the hope that she does not know the full extent of his infamy. She makes it clear by a few hints that he can no longer deceive her. He shows some embarrassment – he bites his lips, and 'hardly knew how to look' (p. 311), but remorse and guilt are not in his vocabulary of behaviour.

Wickham is not a character who changes, but we do learn much more about him as the narrative progresses. His part in the **plot** demonstrates the differences that can exist between appearance and reality. Several times Elizabeth argues that Wickham's good looks prove his honesty; her growing sense of her own foolishness in believing this is a crucial shift in perspective for Elizabeth.

CONTEXT **A04**

Wickham, with his debts, gambling and history of seduction, is revealed as almost the stereotypical rake, a common figure in eighteenth- and early nineteenth-century fiction. The series of paintings and etchings called *The Rake's Progress* by William Hogarth (1697–1764) offers a moralistic view of what happens to such a man, including his downfall. Austen, however, lets Wickham avoid the ignominious end that he justly deserves, by means of the money and generosity of Darcy.

KEY QUOTATION: MR WICKHAM A01

Key quotation:

'But the fact is, that we are very different sort of men, and that he hates me.' (p. 78)

- Volume One, Chapter XVI (Chapter 16), in which Wickham falsely recounts his relationship with Darcy, repays close rereading in comparison with Darcy's true version of the same events in his letter (Volume Two, Chapter XII (Chapter 35)).

- Much of what Wickham says is accurate but the gloss he puts on events is entirely false, and he omits to say anything about the money that Darcy provided and he wasted.

- Of course he says nothing of his plan to elope with Georgiana Darcy.

- With all the skills of a confidence trickster, he is very careful not to tell any direct lies that will be easily detected.

- Elizabeth responds warmly to his version of events – a reaction that cannot escape Wickham, and perhaps emboldens him.

GRADE BOOSTER A02

What are the explicit and implicit moral values which Austen suggests by her plot and characters in *Pride and Prejudice*?

MR COLLINS

WHO IS MR COLLINS?

- William Collins is Mr Bennet's cousin to whom Longbourn will be left after Mr Bennet's death.

- He is a clergyman whose 'living' in Hunsford he owes to his patron, Lady Catherine de Bourgh.

- His manner is pompous and self-important but also very deferential, particularly towards Lady Catherine.

- On meeting the Bennet sisters, he first takes an interest in Jane, then proposes to Elizabeth and three days later proposes to her friend Charlotte Lucas – and is accepted.

A CARICATURE

Mr Collins's character is clear and consistent even from before his very first appearance in the novel. His first letter to Mr Bennet reveals him completely. 'There is something very pompous in his stile … Can he be a sensible man, sir?' (pp. 62–3) Elizabeth asks her father. 'No my dear; I think not. I have great hopes of finding him quite the reverse. There is a mixture of servility and self-importance in his letter which promises well' (p. 63).

At every point Mr Collins lives up to Mr Bennet's **ironic** hopes with his incessant chatter about his attachments to Lady Catherine and Rosings and his irritating catch-phrases – 'the happiest of men' (p. 120), 'humble abode' (p. 153). The utter predictability and triviality of his views and every aspect of his speech brand him as a monster of foolish self-congratulation and something of a **caricature**. He is also frequently so long-winded that Austen has a tendency to sum up his repetitive and boring style of talking via reported speech.

GRADE BOOSTER A02

What do Mr Collins's comments on social activities, such as dancing, backgammon and novel-reading, reveal about his character?

STUDY FOCUS: THE CLERGYMAN   A02

Mr Collins writes to Mr Bennet after hearing of Wickham and Lydia's elopement that 'you certainly ought to forgive them as a christian, but never to admit them in your sight'. '*That* is his notion of christian forgiveness!' comments Mr Bennet (p. 343). Though Wickham might have become a clergyman, Mr Collins is the only actual representative of the Church in *Pride and Prejudice*. He offers several pronouncements on his duties during the novel, but they all revolve around his own self-aggrandising pride and conceit. Austen emphasises his sense of his 'authority as a clergyman, and his rights as a rector' (p. 69), suggesting that the status of clergyman is perhaps more important to Mr Collins than any religious vocation.

KEY QUOTATION: MR COLLINS   A01

Key quotation: 'The death of your daughter would have been a blessing in comparison of this. And it is the more to be lamented, because there is reason to suppose, as my dear Charlotte informs me, that this licentiousness of behaviour in your daughter, has proceeded from a faulty degree of indulgence, though … I am inclined to think that her own disposition must be naturally bad, or she could not be guilty of such an enormity, at so early an age.' (pp. 281–2)

- Mr Collins reveals a cruelly unsympathetic aspect to his character in his letter to the Bennets concerning Lydia's elopement.

- His tone is judgemental and shows a considerable lack of insight, empathy and compassion.

- This quotation demonstrates his trademark verbosity and servility.

- The extremely long second sentence is highly critical of the Bennets but he then attempts, rather insincerely and unsuccessfully, to soften his criticism and console his cousins.

CONTEXT **A04**

Sir William Lucas, in spite of his visits to the Court of St James, is thoroughly in awe of Lady Catherine. Her title indicates her noble birth. The fact that she is called 'Lady Catherine' and not 'Lady de Bourgh' indicates that she is the daughter of an earl (Darcy's grandfather) and not of a mere Baronet like Sir William.

LADY CATHERINE DE BOURGH

WHO IS CATHERINE DE BOURGH?

- Lady Catherine lives at Rosings and is Darcy's aunt and Mr Collins's esteemed patron. She represents the extremes of snobbish pride and prejudice.

- She is high-handed, interfering, rude, overbearing, and infatuated with her position and the justness of her own opinions, many of which are plainly absurd.

- In Volume Three, Chapter XIV (Chapter 56), she pays a visit to Longbourn to attempt to dissuade Elizabeth from accepting Darcy but Elizabeth refuses to be bullied.

RUDENESS AND BREEDING

Learning about her from Mr Collins prepares us for the worst, and when we finally meet Lady Catherine in action at Rosings she fulfils our every expectation. Her claims to excellence in music, for example, are based on nothing but the presumption of her own authority: she does not play yet she offers advice on practice and technique to one and all. When she rudely suggests Elizabeth would not be in the way if she practised on the second-best piano in Rosings, Darcy 'looked a little ashamed of his aunt's ill-breeding' (p. 169). However distinguished her family may be, Austen shows us that her manners are, in their own way, as appalling as Mrs Bennet's. This is one of several ways in which Austen illustrates the idea that manners matter more than social rank in assessing a person's worth.

STUDY FOCUS: THE VISIT TO LONGBOURN · A02

Lady Catherine's visit to Longbourn in Volume Three, Chapter XIV (Chapter 56), to dissuade Elizabeth from accepting Darcy reaches a point almost of farce in its blustering foolishness: 'I came here with the determined resolution of carrying my purpose; nor will I be dissuaded from it' (p. 336). She fails to carry her purpose, and the reader delights in Elizabeth's rational and forceful refusal to be bullied and dominated. It is a neat and **ironic** twist in the **plot** that Lady Catherine's injudicious interference gives Darcy the courage to propose to Elizabeth. Pride and prejudice are defeated at last, and by their own hands.

CHARLOTTE LUCAS

WHO IS CHARLOTTE?

- Charlotte is the twenty-seven-year-old daughter of Sir William and Lady Lucas, neighbours of the Bennets.
- Charlotte and Elizabeth are good friends.
- Charlotte marries Mr Collins, astonishing Elizabeth and putting their friendship under some strain.
- Her views on marriage are realistic and pragmatic.

ENGAGED TO MR COLLINS

Following Elizabeth's rejection of a marriage proposal from Mr Collins, the **narrator** stresses the deliberateness of Charlotte's campaign. When she sees him walking towards the Lucas household, she 'instantly set out to meet him accidentally in the lane' (p. 119). The narrator comments witheringly on Mr Collins's compliance: 'But little had she dared to hope that so much love and eloquence awaited her there' (p. 119).

Elizabeth Bennet is astonished and mortified by Charlotte's agreement to marry Mr Collins. But what kind of future did Charlotte face had she not accepted Mr Collins? Her brothers were 'relieved from their apprehension of Charlotte's dying an old maid' (p. 120). Charlotte's own defence for her decision to marry Mr Collins in Volume One, Chapter XXII (Chapter 22), is that marriage is the 'only honourable provision' (p. 120) for women in her position.

Charlotte's only anxiety concerns Elizabeth's reaction to her decision. As she expects, Elizabeth is shocked. Charlotte's mind is made up but she is as sensitive to Elizabeth's reaction to her marriage as she is about her own feelings in the matter, and she extracts a promise from Elizabeth to visit her in Kent.

LIFE AT HUNSFORD

Volume Two, Chapters V to VII (Chapters 28 to 30), which describe domestic life at Hunsford, must be read carefully to determine whether Charlotte's marriage is 'tolerably happy' (p. 123), or the misery that Elizabeth predicts. Certainly Mr Collins has not changed, and we see Charlotte humouring him with some skill. Likewise she has to suffer the interference of Lady Catherine with good grace. But Elizabeth has 'to give Charlotte credit for the arrangement' of rooms by which she sees relatively little of Mr Collins (p. 164).

STUDY FOCUS: CHARLOTTE'S CLEAR-SIGHTEDNESS A02

Charlotte suspects that Darcy is interested in Elizabeth and 'watched him whenever they were at Rosings' (p. 176); she is alert to this matter, showing her powers of perception to be sharper than Elizabeth's. Clearly there is much that is irksome in Charlotte's new life, but the narrator does not necessarily ask us to accept Elizabeth's view of events. Indeed, in a novel where little is left to the reader's judgement, Austen seems to leave the question open as to Charlotte's 'happiness'.

She certainly shows herself able to tolerate the disadvantages of her existence with dignity and kindness. She is entirely without self-pity. In Mr Collins's final letter to Mr Bennet (Volume Three, Chapter XV (Chapter 57)) we learn that she is pregnant. Do Elizabeth's beauty and wit, and her consequent advantages in the marriage market, blind her to the necessities of Charlotte's situation, or are we led into sharing her easy sense of superiority to her 'very plain' (p. 44) but honest friend? There is a pragmatic and self-interested aspect to love and marriage from which Elizabeth is not wholly immune.

KEY QUOTATION: CHARLOTTE LUCAS   A01

Key quotation: 'She had once or twice suggested to Elizabeth the possibility of [Darcy] being partial to her, but … Mrs Collins did not think it right to press the subject, from the danger of raising expectations which might only end in disappointment; for in her opinion it admitted not of a doubt, that all her friend's dislike would vanish, if she could suppose him to be in her power.' (p. 176)

- Charlotte pragmatically assesses Elizabeth's attitude to Darcy.

- We see her sensitivity to the feelings of her friend in her decision not 'to press the subject' as well as her perceptive insights into the emotional lives of those she cares about.

- She is wrong in the short term as Elizabeth refuses Darcy, and in the long term Elizabeth's love for Darcy grows in proportion to her feeling that he has escaped 'her power'. But the end of the novel shows Charlotte to have been at least partially right.

CRITICAL VIEWPOINT A03

The characterisation of Mr Collins in *Pride and Prejudice* can be seen as cruelly satirical as well as comic. Does his marriage to Charlotte Lucas change our perception of him?

MR AND MRS GARDINER

WHO ARE THE GARDINERS?

- The Gardiners are a happily married couple with four children.
- Mr Gardiner is Mrs Bennet's brother.
- Mrs Gardiner is particularly close to Jane and Elizabeth and offers them good advice.
- They stand for decency, intelligence, good manners and kindness.

NEAR RELATIVES

Elizabeth and Jane desperately need some reasonable relatives, if for nothing else to prove that their own good sense and behaviour is not a genetic impossibility. The Gardiners supply this role in the novel. Surprisingly, the excellent Mr Gardiner is Mrs Bennet's brother. Austen wants to remind us that very near relatives do not necessarily share characteristics, and he is as different from his sister as, say, Elizabeth is from Lydia. Darcy takes to Mr Gardiner instantly at Pemberley, thereby proving his own lack of snobbery: 'It was consoling, that he should know she had some relations for whom there was no need to blush' (p. 244). He looks at the man and not the position in society. Mr Gardiner's home near Cheapside, in sight of his warehouses, was the source of much snobbish humour for Caroline Bingley. Darcy rises above such views.

As characters they are somewhat sketchy. Mr Gardiner likes fishing, and Mrs Gardiner cannot walk very far – but both these traits are there to push the **plot** forward during the Pemberley visit by creating opportunities to meet Darcy. Throughout they have a vital place in the development of the narrative and the **thematic** structure of the book, but we do not learn very much about them.

STUDY FOCUS: WISE ADVICE A02

Mrs Gardiner is required as a wise adviser for the Bennet sisters, to compensate for the silliness of their mother. Elizabeth discusses the nature of Jane's love for Bingley with her (Volume Two, Chapter II (Chapter 25)). She questions Elizabeth about her affection for Wickham (Volume Two, Chapters III and IV (Chapters 26 and 27)). Her letters and suggestions advance the plot: Jane stays with her in London; Elizabeth applies to her to learn why Darcy attended Lydia's wedding; the northern tour results in the fateful visit to Pemberley. Indeed it is a convenience of the plot that Mrs Gardiner should have been brought up near Pemberley, so as to make this a suitable place to visit when their trip to the Lakes falls through.

COLONEL FITZWILLIAM

WHO IS COLONEL FITZWILLIAM?

- Colonel Fitzwilliam is Darcy's cousin.
- As an eligible man, he offers a parallel and contrast to all the other eligible men in *Pride and Prejudice*. He is more immediately charming than Darcy, less apparently charming than Wickham, and, as a younger brother, not wealthy like Bingley.
- He speaks frankly in his conversations with Elizabeth, inadvertently suggesting that Darcy did indeed lure Bingley away from Jane.

MARRIAGE AND MONEY

In Volume Two, Chapter X (Chapter 33), Elizabeth and Fitzwilliam discuss money in a rather open and unemotional way: Colonel Fitzwilliam admits without rancour that 'there are not many in my rank of life who can afford to marry without some attention to money' (p. 179). His comments, and Elizabeth's teasing query about 'what is the usual price of an Earl's younger son?' (p. 180), represent one aspect of the book's anti-romantic examination of the financial basis of marriage.

SISTERS

Pride and Prejudice is a novel about sisters: not only the Bennet sisters but others too.

THE BINGLEY SISTERS

Bingley has two sisters. The reader is told almost nothing about Mrs Hurst, the older sister; we presume that her husband, whose chief interest is food, has married her for her money. His younger sister Caroline Bingley enters into the **plot** as a false friend to Jane and a rival to Elizabeth in Darcy's affections, though Darcy appears to feel nothing but polite contempt for her advances.

Caroline participates in all the conversations at Netherfield when Darcy is forming an agreeable impression of Elizabeth. In these she stands for snobbery, unsubtle flattery of Darcy (as opposed to Elizabeth's wit and detachment) and jealousy. She offers a parallel and contrast to Elizabeth in their modes of conversation and courtship (since all conversations between unmarried men and women seem to involve an element of flirtation, grave or frivolous according to the persons involved).

Though she had encouraged Jane to visit Netherfield, she decides that her brother must be detached from Jane (and Elizabeth kept away from Darcy), and so she is instrumental in Bingley's sudden departure from Hertfordshire. Jane wants to believe in Caroline Bingley as a friend, but receives the cold shoulder from her in London, and has to admit that Elizabeth's cynical view of her behaviour has proved correct (in her letter in Volume Two, Chapter III (Chapter 26)).

GEORGIANA DARCY

Darcy's sister, Georgiana, is required in the novel's plot for a number of reasons. Caroline Bingley wants her brother to marry her, or at least this idea is offered as an obstacle to Jane's love for Bingley. Georgiana's near elopement with Wickham implicates Darcy in Lydia's elopement. Darcy's desire to introduce Georgiana to Elizabeth when they meet at Pemberley in Volume Three, Chapter III (Chapter 45) is a strong compliment and a clear indication of respect: 'Elizabeth saw that he was anxious for his sister and herself to get acquainted, and forwarded, as much as possible, every attempt at conversation on either side' (p. 257). Georgiana herself is characterised as shy, and her shyness is mistaken for

GRADE BOOSTER A02

Examine the theme of sisterhood in *Pride and Prejudice*, paying attention to minor characters as well as to Jane and Elizabeth.

pride: is this a hint at Darcy's character? Her almost fearful respect for her older brother is contrasted with Elizabeth's playful wifely behaviour in the final summing-up of the plot.

MARIA LUCAS

The Lucases' younger daughter, Maria, is a foil for Elizabeth in their visit to Charlotte at Hunsford. Her innocent awe at the grandeur of Lady Catherine and Rosings and her ordinary interest in the domestic affairs of her sister, Charlotte, offer a contrast to Elizabeth's self-reliance and sophistication, and perhaps her cynicism.

SERVANTS

Servants in *Pride and Prejudice* are characterised more by their silence and anonymity than by their explicit presence in the text. However, the modern reader needs to be reminded that they are always there in the dining and drawing rooms of every house, as witnesses to the action. In Longbourn, a relatively modest household, the following servants are mentioned: the housekeeper, two housemaids, a butler and a footman. But there would probably have been more in such a household, and of course there were all the agricultural workers required on the estate, as well as staff to manage the horses and carriage. Sometimes the knowledge of servants is a source of embarrassment, as, for example, when the news of Lydia's elopement spreads: '"Oh, Jane!" cried Elizabeth, "was there a servant … who did not know the whole story by the end of the day?"' (p. 277).

The housekeepers of Longbourn and Pemberley are mentioned by name (Mrs Hill and Mrs Reynolds), and they play a small part in the plot. Mrs Reynolds provides a surprising view of Darcy's good temper and absolute honour. Though the Gardiners and Elizabeth start by feeling that her views are the exaggerations of a fond old retainer, they are finally convinced that her admiration for Darcy does in fact bear witness to his true character: 'What praise is more valuable than the praise of an intelligent servant?' (p. 240). Mrs Hill is indispensable during the crisis of Lydia's disappearance, when Mrs Bennet takes to her bed in despairing hysterics; we can only imagine what might be her view of the Bennet household, and its master and mistress.

Only the ill-behaved Lydia shows any interest in the appearance of servants: 'that is just like your formality and discretion. You thought the waiter must not hear, as if he cared! I dare say he often hears worse things than I am going to say. But he is an ugly fellow! I am glad he is gone. I never saw such a long chin in my life' (p. 212). Such remarks are strong indications of her lack of decorum.

> **CHECK THE FILM** A04
>
> The BBC version makes clear the way servants are everywhere and ever-present in the lives of Austen's characters.

THEMES

CHARACTER AS A THEME

THE STUDY OF CHARACTER

The word 'character' refers to an imaginary person in a literary text; it can also be used to refer to personality, to the particular attitudes and behaviours that make people different from each other. An interest in this psychological individuality is touched upon at various points in the novel. 'I did not know before,' Bingley says to Elizabeth, 'that you were a studier of character. It must be an amusing study' (p. 42). Darcy asks her why she is asking so many questions. 'Merely to the illustration of *your* character', she replies; 'I am trying to make it out' (p. 92). Easy-going Bingley is easily understood; Darcy, however, is more complicated.

WILL AND REASON

We may consider Austen's range of **characterisation** in terms of this struggle between will and reason, desire and sense, and the realisation of truths. Some characters are the victims of their feelings and desires. Lydia, for example, simply follows her will. Her behaviour is untempered by reason or reasonableness: her morals and manners are deplorable. Mrs Bennet is completely the victim of her immediate feelings, which simply flow through her conversation unchecked. It is plainly wrong to be the victim of one's feelings, and it seems a sign of excellence to be involved in the kind of battles to control and understand themselves that Darcy and Elizabeth undergo. However, *Pride and Prejudice* seems to argue that to possess these strong feelings in the first place is also creditable. Jane and Bingley nearly lose each other because Jane conceals her feelings, and Bingley can be persuaded to leave her by Darcy and his sisters. Mr Bennet's feelings and moral convictions are lost in the play of his **irony** and cynicism.

ON REFLECTION

Often in Jane Austen's novels we are shown the more reflective individuals overcoming powerful feelings and obstinate prejudices. Elizabeth is shown on several occasions battling with herself, moderating her feelings by the processes of thinking rationally about them, or realising truths that she has formerly denied. Her response and steady change of attitude when she receives Darcy's letter is a notable example of this. Having prided herself on her ability to understand characters, she is furious when she finds herself to be entirely in the wrong with regard to Darcy and Wickham: 'I, who have prided myself on my discernment … How humiliating is this discovery! … I have courted prepossession and ignorance, and driven reason away … Till this moment, I never knew myself' (p. 201–2).

STUDY FOCUS: WHAT IS MEANT BY 'CHARACTER'? A02

A comment of Elizabeth's may help the reader in identifying exactly what is meant by a person's character. Her anger is sparked off by Darcy's tactless account of his efforts to avoid falling in love with her: 'you chose to tell me that you liked me against your will, against your reason, and even against your character' (p. 186). This is a traditional view, opposing 'will' against 'reason': we are pulled in one direction by our desires, but we moderate them by our reason. In her analysis, character is seen as a separate entity. Her qualifying 'character' with 'even' suggests that Darcy has more control over this element in his make-up than over his will or reason. This suggests that 'character' is the deliberate, self-conscious and observable manner with which Darcy deals with the world. 'Character' would seem to be the collection of choices that an individual makes in the constant battle between desire and rational compromise. It is not simply 'manners': Wickham's manners may be perfect but his actions reveal his real character.

CONTEXT A04

In thinking about Austen's view of character, it might be worth remembering that in the early nineteenth century psychology, the scientific investigation of the mind and personality, was not as it is now, a specialised field of study that we take for granted. Ideas about the nature of human character were the province of philosophy, poetry and the novel. The psychoanalyst Sigmund Freud, a pioneer in the study of the mind, was born in 1856 and his groundbreaking studies, such as *The Interpretation of Dreams*, were published at the start of the twentieth century.

PRIDE AND PREJUDICE

CLASS AND WEALTH

Pride and prejudice are the explicit **themes** that Austen chooses to place as the title of her novel. Austen writes at a point of social change, and one area in which pride is seen to prevail is in the differences of class and wealth between characters. In her hierarchical worldview and condescending manner, Catherine de Bourgh may be seen to embody pride and prejudice. Mr Collins has absorbed Lady Catherine's vision of the world and is proud to be associated with her in every respect. It is noticeable how the narrator suggests nothing but contempt for these two persons, who are demeaned as **caricatures**. They are shown as unwaveringly and ludicrously proud and stupid.

DARCY'S PRIDE

Darcy is proud. Charlotte Lucas, often the mouthpiece for interesting opinions at odds with Elizabeth's, remarks that his pride 'does not offend *me* so much as pride often does, because there is an excuse for it … If I may so express it, he has a *right* to be proud' (p. 21). Darcy himself says that 'where there is a real superiority of mind, pride will always be under good regulation' (p. 56), which makes Elizabeth smile, because she thinks his pride unregulated. The novel as a whole shows Darcy learning to regulate his pride appropriately, and to recognise that Elizabeth is not irredeemably tainted by the Bennet family's social position and behaviour. He must also learn to bury these prejudices when he addresses himself to Elizabeth.

ELIZABETH'S PREJUDICE

The novel also shows us Elizabeth coming to terms with her prejudice against Darcy. She makes up her mind about him too quickly, based on his rude and stand-offish behaviour at the first dance at which he appears in Meryton, when he remarks that 'she is not handsome enough to tempt *me*' (p. 13). Elizabeth's first impressions lead her astray. In her misjudgement of Wickham's character, she is taken in by his handsome appearance. The novel teaches us that the ordinary human prejudice in favour of a handsome appearance and a charming manner is not to be trusted.

> **GRADE BOOSTER**
>
> Analyse the different attitudes to pride expressed through the characters and action of *Pride and Prejudice*.

STUDY FOCUS: SOCIAL MOBILITY A02

Pride and Prejudice shows how the ancient families of land-owning gentry are having to come to terms with new, mobile, wealthy middle-class families whose fortunes have been made by trade. Some, like Lady Catherine de Bourgh, cannot accept the way in which new class boundaries are having to be drawn. Darcy's marriage to Elizabeth Bennet will result in a link between her family and Wickham, but it is Wickham's origins as much as his bad character that make her furious at this possibility. 'I am no stranger to the particulars of your youngest sister's infamous elopement … is *such* a girl to be my nephew's sister? Is *her* husband, is the son of his late father's steward, to be his brother? … Are the shades of Pemberley to be thus polluted?' (p. 338).

MARRIAGE

There are four courtships leading to marriage for the reader to consider in the course of *Pride and Prejudice*, as well as two more established marriages which are opened up to our scrutiny.

CHARLOTTE AND MR COLLINS

Charlotte Lucas and Mr Collins are the first 'lovers' to arrive at marriage in the novel. Charlotte's reasons for marrying the repellant Mr Collins are explained in the section on her character above. Charlotte's life at Hunsford poses the question: what is the nature of a 'successful' marriage?

LYDIA AND WICKHAM

Lydia and Wickham start by living together. His interest in Lydia is, it seems, sexual; she is infatuated by his appearance. Both are shamelessly uncaring about the disgrace that their immorality has caused the Bennet family. Wickham is persuaded into marriage by a financial package. Austen presents their union as a model for a bad marriage, characterised by a lack of love, integrity and money.

CRITICAL VIEWPOINT A03

Explore the tensions in *Pride and Prejudice* between 'the ebullience and confident assurance of its comedy, combined with its fairy-tale gratification' (Isobel Armstrong) and the novel's constant preoccupation with money.

JANE AND BINGLEY

Jane and Bingley represent the coming-together of two handsome, like-minded and kind-hearted persons. Their eventual marriage is delightful but perhaps not as passionate as Elizabeth and Darcy's. It is doubtful that their separation, for which they are partly responsible, has deepened their understanding of themselves or each other. But since they are so well matched this scarcely matters.

ELIZABETH AND DARCY

Elizabeth and Darcy have to overcome his pride and her disdainful dislike of him in order to realise their love. In doing this they both change considerably, and they have to learn hard lessons about their own inadequacies of character and understanding. But they also learn about each other and their respective qualities in times of stress. Theirs is a marriage of opposites. Her liveliness and mischievous pleasure in the oddities of human behaviour are combined with his self-conscious gravity and decency. This mutual knowledge, the pattern of the novel suggests, makes their marriage the strongest and most interesting of all.

MR AND MRS BENNET

The Bennets' marriage is shown to us throughout the novel, and is explained by the narrator late on in the narrative, at the start of Volume Two, Chapter XIX (Chapter 42). It is a picture of a bad marriage: 'Respect, esteem and confidence, had vanished for ever' (p. 228). When Mr Bennet questions Elizabeth at length about her feelings for Darcy, he shows true responsibility, and a sense of the pain behind his **irony** emerges: 'My child, let me not have the grief of seeing *you* unable to respect your partner in life' (p. 356).

THE GARDINERS

The Gardiners are an amiable couple with a brood of lively children. The novel ends with a compliment to them, as the persons who by bringing Elizabeth to Derbyshire had brought her and Darcy together. This is true in terms of the plot, but in a larger way the Gardiners illustrate the benefits and blessings of marriage itself. The institution of marriage, to which all the characters in the novel devote themselves with relative success or failure, is upheld by the Gardiners. The happiness of a wise marriage is perhaps the 'truth universally acknowledged' (p. 5) that hovers over *Pride and Prejudice*. For Austen and her sensible characters, nothing matters more.

KEY QUOTATION: MARRIAGE A01

Key quotation: 'Happy for all her maternal feelings was the day on which Mrs Bennet got rid of her two most deserving daughters. With what delighted pride she afterwards visited Mrs Bingley and talked of Mrs Darcy may be guessed.' (p. 364)

- The last chapter of the novel shows that the problem that preoccupied Mrs Bennet in the first chapter has been resolved.
- The phrase 'got rid' reminds the reader of Mrs Bennet's desperation to find eligible husbands for her daughters.
- The novel has made clear, however, that marriage is about 'connubial felicity' (p. 296) in the long term, not merely 'elegant nuptials' (p. 294). The remainder of this final chapter gives us some insights into her daughters' marriages in their first year or so.

LOVE

WHAT IS LOVE?

Love in *Pride and Prejudice* often has to do with marriage. The novel shows it to be a state of rhapsodical admiration into which young men pass before making their proposals: Darcy does this twice, Bingley once, while Mr Collins pays lip-service to the idea of being in love. Austen depicts love as usually a secret, internalised, almost shameful state of mind: the victims above start by expressing admiration and liking, but then have to blurt out the word.

DISPLAYING OR CONCEALING ONE'S FEELINGS

Love can be concealed from everyone, even from one's closest family and friends. Jane, Elizabeth's confidante in everything, is astonished to hear of Elizabeth's feelings for Darcy.

The object of such feeling is often in a state of ignorance too, as Bingley is of Jane's love for him. Charlotte believes it useful to display these feelings so as to leave no one in doubt. The events of the novel suggest there might have been wisdom in this view for Jane and Elizabeth. In Charlotte's own case there is no love for Mr Collins to conceal, but she is equally open and active in her agreement to his business arrangement.

Trying to spot where people's affections really lie is a pastime indulged by many characters in the book. Mrs Gardiner warns Elizabeth about her growing attachment to Wickham and later looks in vain for clues to her feelings towards Darcy. Caroline Bingley ruthlessly teases Darcy about his admiration for Elizabeth's 'fine eyes'.

STUDY FOCUS: MISMATCHED FEELINGS A02

Unrequited love, like Jane's for Bingley (or so she fears), is an undesirable state of mind in itself – we feel nothing but sympathy for Jane's suffering. Things are worse if it is a matter of public knowledge, as it is for Jane. Elizabeth keeps her growing but seemingly futile interest in Darcy secret with good reason. Much of the comedy of the novel involves a mismatch of feeling between lovers, and misunderstandings caused by how lovers appear in public compared to the private reality of their feelings. It is ironic that Darcy takes Bingley away from Jane because he thinks she is not in love with him (while Bingley is falling in love with her), and then himself proposes to Elizabeth when she detests him.

GRADE BOOSTER A02

All of Austen's novels examine the nature of love and marriage. For short synopses of her other novels – and to find out more about the importance of love and marriage in those works – look online.

CHECK THE BOOK A03

Read Austen's *Persuasion* (1818) for another, less comical study of concealed and eventually requited love.

MONEY AND SELF-INTEREST

FINANCIAL IMPROPRIETY

Charlotte remarks of herself, 'I am not romantic you know' (p. 123). Neither is the narrator of *Pride and Prejudice*. This is a love story, but one in which passion is tempered by sensible thoughts about money. Lydia does not lack passion in her admiration for Wickham. In some novels, to throw caution to the winds and run away with a handsome young officer would be the very emblem of thrillingly passionate behaviour. In this novel it is severely condemned. The financial fecklessness of Wickham is as strong a mark against him as his sexual immorality.

WEALTH, PROPERTY AND SECURITY

So careful is the narrator to give financial details of almost every significant character in *Pride and Prejudice*, that money emerges as am important **theme** of the novel.

When Elizabeth comments to Jane that her love for Darcy began 'from my first seeing his beautiful grounds at Pemberley' (p. 353), what element of truthfulness is there in this? She feels 'some perturbation' on approaching Pemberley: 'her spirits were in a high flutter' (p. 235). When she sees the estate (the only piece of sustained topographical description in the book, and therefore **foregrounded**), 'at that moment she felt, that to be mistress of Pemberley might be something!' (p. 235). She speaks of a present and a future, not of something past and concluded. It is not 'to have been' but 'to be'. Darcy's wealth is of great interest to Elizabeth, when she is confronted by its reality.

The women of the Bennet family are in real financial difficulty. When Mr Bennet dies, they lose their home and the income attached to it. Even a stickler for old ways like Lady Catherine regards the entailment of property down through male relatives, excluding wives and daughters, to be unnecessary (not least because it would have deprived her of Rosings). There is a hard and unsentimental reality to almost every aspect of this comedy of courtship and marriage.

STUDY FOCUS: CHARLOTTE'S 'KIND SCHEMES' A02

Charlotte Collins, thinking up 'kind schemes' (p. 177) for Elizabeth, feels that Colonel Fitzwilliam was 'beyond comparison the pleasantest man; he certainly admired her, and his situation in life was most eligible; but, to counterbalance these advantages, Mr Darcy had considerable patronage in the church and his cousin could have none at all' (p. 177). Placing this at the end of a chapter emphasises the final twist, in which Charlotte's thoughts move from the outcome that might suit her friend best, to that which would serve her own purposes through the advancement and enrichment of Mr Collins. We are tempted into laughing at the way Charlotte's fanciful speculations come down to earth in self-interest.

REVISION FOCUS: TASK 4 A03

How far do you agree with the following statements?

- Financial prudence is an important virtue in *Pride and Prejudice*.
- The words 'pride' and 'prejudice' can be applied to a number of characters in the novel.

Write opening paragraphs for essays based on these discussion points. Set out your arguments clearly.

LUCK AND HAPPINESS

COINCIDENCE AND CHANCE

Inherent in the **plot** of *Pride and Prejudice* is a debate about the nature of luck and the role that luck plays in bringing about happiness. There is a pattern of circumstances and events that is outside the control of the characters, but which is essential in the furthering of the narrative. It is good luck that Mrs Gardiner was brought up near Pemberley, that Mr Gardiner's business interests curtail the time available for the proposed Lake District tour so that Elizabeth and the Gardiners visit Derbyshire, and that Darcy should return to Pemberley earlier than expected and therefore bump into Elizabeth.

Charlotte Lucas remarks that 'Happiness in marriage is entirely a matter of chance' (p. 24), and the plot of the novel demonstrates that chance certainly plays its part in bringing a solution to the apparent stalemate in the marital hopes of the two Bennet sisters.

CREDIBILITY

None of these events in themselves stretches our credulity too far. All are realistic and likely, and Austen is not suggesting anything providential or mystical in the bringing together of the would-be lovers. Indeed, the motive for the visit is Mrs Gardiner's (and eventually Elizabeth's) very strong curiosity to see round the house and grounds. Nonetheless, an implicit suggestion in this arrangement is that chance plays a strong part in human fortune.

> **GRADE BOOSTER** A02
>
> How much does the plot of *Pride and Prejudice* demonstrate the truth of Charlotte Lucas's assertion that 'Happiness in marriage is entirely a matter of chance' (p. 24)?

WOMEN'S ROLE

WOMEN'S POINT OF VIEW

To what degree does Austen specifically address the issues facing women in the society she depicts in her novels? This is a question that many critics have addressed in the last decades and to which a variety of answers have been put forward. There is plenty of evidence to consider in *Pride and Prejudice*. It is a woman's perception of events that we are shown: it is a commonplace of Austen criticism that men are never shown away from the company of women. We are shown sisters, aunts and female confidantes exchanging views, discussing events and sharing secrets. In the course of these discussions, and in the unfolding events of the novel, many different points of view about the role of women in marriage are expressed, from Mrs Bennet's obsessive planning to Mr Bennet's disdain for his wife's trivial interests.

ELIZABETH'S STRENGTH OF CHARACTER

The nature of a good marriage seems the novel's major **theme**, and Austen does not present in a positive light any possible role for educated young women other than marriage. But Elizabeth's narrative, while ending in marriage, presents a **protagonist** notable for her independence of mind and the spirited freedom of her thinking about her world, even in spite of the pressures caused by its narrowness, snobbery and the straitjacket of its conventions. Darcy calls this 'liveliness of mind' and she brands it 'impudence' when at the book's end they look back on their early conversations: 'you were sick of civility, of deference, of officious attention. You were disgusted with the women who were always speaking and looking, and thinking of *your* approbation alone. I roused, and interested you, because I was so unlike *them*' (p. 359). Her desirability rests in her intelligence and charisma, rather than any set of accomplishments that can be learned.

Elizabeth controls the conversations at Netherfield, and always dominates Darcy in conversation, often drawing attention to his broody silences. She tells her father in vain that Lydia should be controlled. She stands up to Lady Catherine. She breaks the silence between herself and Darcy by thanking him for his secret generosity to Lydia. Within the limits of her situation she is an extremely strong young woman. But her strength does not go beyond the conventional propriety of a daughter and wife; duty to family and husband remains central to the female agenda.

CHECK THE BOOK A03

See **Critical debates: Feminist criticism** and **Further reading** for some suggestions of titles to investigate among the many feminist critics who have written about Jane Austen's novels.

STUDY FOCUS: SUITABLE PASTIMES FOR YOUNG LADIES A02

In Volume One, Chapter VIII (Chapter 8), there is a discussion of the 'accomplishments' of young ladies. Bingley is all admiration for their ability to 'paint tables, cover skreens and net purses' (p. 39). Darcy wants more than this, and more even than the list Caroline Bingley provides of 'music, singing, drawing, dancing and the modern languages' plus 'something in her air and manner of walking' (p. 39). To all these Darcy adds 'the improvement of her mind by extensive reading' (p. 39). We know nothing of Elizabeth's reading, though Darcy attempts to draw her into discussing books at the Netherfield ball. She can sing and play the piano but, to Lady Catherine's astonishment, does not draw. At the novel's end, Mary Bennet seems to be heading for an unmarried

life looking after her mother, but her character and learning are not rendered admirable during the book. Indeed, the **narrator** suggests somewhat cruelly that her studies were a strategy to make up for her lack of beauty.

PART FOUR: STRUCTURE, FORM AND LANGUAGE

STRUCTURE

STORYTELLING

The events of *Pride and Prejudice* are recounted in **chronological order**. Austen uses narration, conversation and letters to provide supplementary background information about characters; this information is inserted into the main narrative in a natural and timely way and can have a huge impact on the way the characters and the reader view events. The structure of the novel is presented to the reader as the structure of the characters' lives: we observe the months and seasons change, the anticipation leading up to key events such as dinners and balls in the social calendar, and the impact on the neighbourhood of 'news' about, for example, the tenant of Netherfield or the arrival of the militia at Meryton. At times, Austen deliberately describes a lull in the Bennet household – 'With no greater events than these in the Longbourn family … did January and February pass away' (p.149) – but Austen's momentum as a storyteller is never lost.

HAPPY EVER AFTER

Love and marriage play a key part in governing the narrative structure and pacing of *Pride and Prejudice*. We may see the happy endings as inevitable from the very beginning and rightly anticipate that there will be obstacles and misunderstandings along the way. Although we may anticipate the outcome for Elizabeth and Darcy, the intricacies of how that outcome is reached have absorbed generations of readers, delighted by the novel's energetic pace and drive, its blending of seriousness and comedy, and the elegance and sureness of the narrative voice.

There is no sense of things unfolding chaotically in Austen's novels. We sense from the first pages of the text that she knows where events are leading, and that everything we are being told or shown may be significant and somehow related to the final outcome of events. This strong impression of control and her capacity to judge and mock her characters suggests the presence of someone highly intelligent, who can skilfully present the follies of human nature in the context of a satisfying love story.

THREE VOLUMES

The novel is structured in three volumes, a standard form of publishing in the nineteenth century. The three volumes can be compared to the acts of a play, with each section concluding dramatically. In *Pride and Prejudice*, Volume One ends with Charlotte accepting Mr Collins's hand in marriage, Mrs Bennet 'really in a most pitiable state' (p. 27) and with growing concerns about Bingley's ever returning to Netherfield. Volume Two concludes with Elizabeth's curiosity about her impending visit to Pemberley with the Gardiners. Volume Three of course concludes with the marriages of Elizabeth and Jane and the tying up of loose ends.

CONTEXT A04

Publication of novels in three separately bound volumes was very common in the nineteenth century. A reader could borrow a single volume from a library and return to borrow the next. Novels could also be enjoyed by more than one family member at a time.

FORM

REALISM

In *Pride and Prejudice*, Austen is not interested in description for its own sake, and her vocabulary is distinguished by the predominance of abstract words. So it is perhaps odd to insist that her chosen mode of writing is **realism**. This has to do as much with the milieu and manners she chooses to write about as the way in which she writes about them. Meryton is recognisably an ordinary society not unlike that inhabited by her original readers. She does not describe a fantasy world. There are no haunted ruins, dungeons or castles; no mad monks or man-made monsters. In other words, this is not a **Gothic** novel, in which the pleasure consists of entering a world quite unlike our own ordinary existence, where feelings and passions are stretched to excess, far beyond the key values of Austen's society: propriety, amiability, civility.

THE NARRATOR

OMNISCIENT NARRATOR

Pride and Prejudice is told to us by an anonymous and **omniscient narrator**. Sometimes the narrator is the silent observer of events, relating them without comment. At other times we are told quite clearly what to think about a character or an incident. An obvious feature of the narrative are those passages of summary, often at the beginning or the end of a chapter, when the narrator takes command and offers opinions or sums up aspects of the characters. These are sharply different in tone and **style** from passages that describe the incidents and events of the novel. Often the difference lies in the way in which time is handled. The moving present of the action is described as it happens, while reflections that depart from this moving present involve the narrator generalising or summarising.

CHECK THE BOOK A04

Austen's *Northanger Abbey* (1818) incorporates and mocks elements of the popular Gothic novel.

A narrator who summarises and comments (not all narrators do this: some try to be entirely anonymous) to some extent has the same kind of existence for us as a character in the novel. In some novels – though not in this one – we come to regard the narrative voice as less than completely trustworthy. We have to stand back and see that the way the story is being told is partial or from a particular and limited perspective. There are examples of a partial view of events in *Pride and Prejudice*, but not to the extent that we would regard the narrator as unreliable. For example, we are not immediately told all we need to know about Darcy and Wickham's past so we are, like Elizabeth, liable to judge the merit of these two men quite wrongly. If we had known more, then we could have enjoyed knowingly watching her make her mistakes, rather than learning from events as she does. To this extent the narrator enjoys mildly tricking her readers.

In her summaries the narrator is judgemental. She sometimes mocks her characters. This places her above the comic world she describes. Her summarising authorial comment on characters can be ferociously direct and critical – Mrs Bennet's ignorance, for example, at the end of the first chapter.

CENTRE OF CONSCIOUSNESS

As the novel develops, we tend to be shown events from Elizabeth's point of view, using her as a **centre of consciousness**. We do witness conversations in which she does not participate, for example when Bingley's sisters comment on her appearance behind her back in Volume One, Chapter VIII (Chapter 8). And even towards the end of the novel, the narrator will tell us quite unexpectedly what another character, such as Mrs Gardiner, is thinking. However, large stretches of the novel are given over to the attempt to reproduce the contents of Elizabeth's consciousness as she modifies her view of Darcy from settled dislike to love. One of the narrative techniques used

to achieve this is **free indirect discourse** ('Oh! Why did she come', p. 241), which is midway between direct speech or thought ("Oh! Why did I come?"), and reported speech or thought ('she wondered why she had come'). Free indirect discourse is used throughout the novel and suggests Austen's determination to display the psychological processes of her **protagonist**.

GRADE BOOSTER   **A02**

Examine the narrator's stance and presence in *Pride and Prejudice* by careful analysis of several passages.

STUDY FOCUS: A FEMALE PERSPECTIVE?   **A02**

It would be perverse to call the narrator of *Pride and Prejudice* 'he'. But for the purposes of discussing all the effects of the text, we should not simply assume that this narrator *is* Jane Austen. Is there any aspect of the text that would mark the narrator as female? She has a sharp (and critical) eye for female fashion, though little is said about the clothes

themselves. She is equally clear-sighted about carriages, and money (but then so are many of the women in the book). She seems to despise many of the female characters' foibles, some of which might be regarded as gender-specific. But she is equally harsh on the inadequacy and pomposity of her male characters. The spheres of activity in the novel are those in which women are always present. Men are never shown outside the company of women. It might be argued that the main **theme** of the novel, marriage, suggests a female perspective; but of course men are equally involved in the business of wedlock, and in the novel they have much to learn from their mistakes.

CRITICAL VIEWPOINT   **A03**

Do you agree that the narrator of *Pride and Prejudice* is judgemental?

REVISION FOCUS: TASK 5   **A03**

How far do you agree with the following statements?

● Austen's omniscient narration is judgemental but even-handed; she exposes weaknesses and flaws in each of her characters.

● Despite the obstacles they have to overcome, Austen shows Elizabeth and Darcy to be well-matched suitors from the beginning of the novel.

Write opening paragraphs for essays based on these discussion points. Set out your arguments clearly.

LETTERS

The exchange of letters in *Pride and Prejudice* makes it clear that the English postal service in the early nineteenth century was reasonably reliable and even swift. Letters were expensive, and were paid for by the receiver rather than the sender of the letter. Mail coaches, introduced in 1784, joined the major cities in a regular service, and were available also as transport for ordinary travellers. Elizabeth uses the post in this way to return from her visit to Charlotte Lucas in Hunsford.

Fay Weldon's *Letters to Alice On First Reading Jane Austen* (1984) is a modern **epistolary** work, in which a woman writes to her niece about literature, writing and the relevance and pleasures of reading Jane Austen's novels in modern times.

Pride and Prejudice contains some forty letters, their contents reported or reproduced in their entirety. Many of the eighteenth-century English novels that Austen read, such as *Clarissa* (1748) by Samuel Richardson (see left) and *Evelina* (1778) by Fanny Burney, are **epistolary novels**, consisting entirely of letters. Such a method of writing a novel was not at all unusual in the early nineteenth century. *First Impressions*, the lost original of *Pride and Prejudice*, was probably constructed in this way. In *Pride and Prejudice* letters are part of the text's verisimilitude. They feel authentic and help to establish a closeness between character and reader.

Letter-writing is a serious business for characters like Darcy, Jane, and Mr and Mrs Gardiner. Contrastingly, Lydia's effusions are skimpy and trivial or shamelessly self-interested, as in her application for money in the last chapter. Mr Bennet is a lazy letter-writer; his are infrequent and short. Letters provide a way of distinguishing character. Mr Collins is recognised as a buffoon from his first letter. Darcy's letter of explanation to Elizabeth is a crucial text in itself: 'she was in a fair way of soon knowing it by heart. She studied every sentence: and her feelings towards its writer were at times widely different' (p. 206). Anyone who doubts the variety of Austen's capacities as a writer should compare the different styles of the letters in *Pride and Prejudice*.

LANGUAGE

STYLE

DESCRIPTION AND ABSTRACTION

Jane Austen's **style** seems more reminiscent of the prose-writers of the eighteenth century than of the Romantic poets who were her contemporaries. There are very few descriptive passages. What is in the text is there for a purpose: there is no painting in words, no description for its own sake.

There are indeed relatively few **concrete nouns** in *Pride and Prejudice*. A few objects spring to mind – carriages, a muddy petticoat, several hats, pictures, a parasol, pyramids of grapes, nectarines and peaches that provide a welcome distraction during an embarrassing social occasion. Such things as are mentioned serve an immediate purpose. Austen is not interested in visualising the world she describes, except in special cases, like Pemberley. This applies also to the appearance of her characters.

A far larger proportion of nouns in Austen's prose deal with abstractions and generalities, with ideas and feelings. Open any page and **abstract nouns** are almost everywhere: astonishment, pride, sense, judgement, hope, etc.

STUDY FOCUS: FIGURATIVE LANGUAGE **A02**

There is little or no **metaphor** in *Pride and Prejudice*. There is, however, one kind of **figurative language** which relates Austen to prose writers of the middle and late eighteenth century such as Dr Johnson. This is the structuring of her sentences and arrangement of words so as to create a sense of balance, pattern and proportion. In the following case, the linguistic cleverness is ascribed to Elizabeth, who is thinking about Charlotte: 'her home, and her housekeeping, her parish and her poultry, and all their dependent concerns, had not yet lost their charms' (p. 209). The alliteration draws attention to the two pairs of words. 'Home' and 'housekeeping' fit together well, though the first suggests positive, warm values, the second concerns money and work. 'Parish' widens the concerns away from the parsonage to a wider scope of responsibility, but 'poultry' rather than finishing the list with a final grand idea, ends on a note of **bathos**; by the **antithesis** between these ideas, Charlotte's concerns are finally condemned as narrow and trivial.

IRONY

IRONIC COMMENTS

The **narrator** loves to make **ironic** comments about some of her characters. In Volume One, Chapter XXII (Chapter 22), Charlotte Lucas is worried that Mr Collins will have to depart from Hertfordshire before her scheme can succeed: 'but here, she did injustice to the *fire and independence of his character*, for it led him to escape out of Longbourn House the next morning with admirable slyness, and hasten to Lucas Lodge *to throw himself at her feet*' (p. 119; italics added). Such fire and passion, though exaggerated, are the opposite of all that we know of Mr Collins, and we take pleasure in the inappropriateness of the description. The narrator may be indicating the language that Mr Collins might himself use to aggrandise his activities, but the effect is still ironically amusing. We know that we are not to accept the description at its face value.

Occasionally Elizabeth indulges in malicious irony. '*I like her appearance*', she says on seeing Miss De Bourgh for the first time, but then she explains what is so pleasing: 'she looks

GRADE BOOSTER **A02**

Irony, since it consists of saying one thing while meaning another, runs the risk of being incomprehensible unless writer and reader, or speaker and listener, share a common code of values. Elizabeth understands Mr Bennet's ironies, while her mother and younger sisters do not. We come to understand Austen's values through the experience of reading her work. Consider the ironies inherent in the novel's opening sentence ('It is a truth universally acknowledged …') in the light of the whole novel.

sickly and cross. – Yes, she will do very well for him' (p. 156; italics added). In **irony** of this kind, we need to know something that lies outside the immediate sentence in order to understand what is meant. In the first case we have to know Mr Collins for the calculating and pompous man that he is, to understand that the description of his actions is inappropriate. In the second, we soon learn Elizabeth does not like Miss De Bourgh's appearance at all, except in so far as it fuels her dislike for Darcy. The danger of saying something that you do not mean is that unless your audience shares your point of view, they may miss the point entirely. As readers we have to be perpetually on our guard, to pick up the ironies or miss the point.

IRONY AND ATTITUDE

Examples so far have shown irony as a feature of language, but irony can be as much a way of thinking as a technique. The word 'ironic' is used to describe the ability to see things from several points of view. In this respect Austen's writing is always ironic. She likes to present mutually incompatible points of view. This is true of her treatment of her largest **themes** and incidents. A central irony of the novel is that Darcy proposes to Elizabeth, who at this stage detests him.

The narrator shares an ironic enjoyment of the activities of her characters with Mr Bennet and with Elizabeth. Mr Bennet's irony is constant and public. Elizabeth rarely exercises her irony in this way at the expense of others, and where she does so in public it is in the form of a playful conversational exchange, part of her love for **paradox**, rather than as a way of indulging in the superiority of private detachment. Darcy is the chief butt of this kind of wit, and he is intelligent enough to know the nature of Elizabeth's game, and follow the play of her ideas, even when he is under attack.

CHECK THE BOOK A03

Norman Page's *The Language of Jane Austen* (1972) is a full-scale study; the same author writes a chapter on Austen's language in *The Jane Austen Handbook* edited by J. David Grey (1986).

CHECK THE BOOK A03

Typical eighteenth-century satirical writing relies on a shared foundation of values in author and audience in order to be comprehensible. Try reading some of Pope's 'Epistle II. To A Lady: Of the Characters of Women' (1735). The poet criticises what he regards as the folly of the world, assuming the reader has a shared understanding of what is 'common sense'. Is this true of Jane Austen's **irony**?

HISTORICAL BACKGROUND

WAR WITH FRANCE

The officers of the militia are conscripts. In other words, it is a non-professional regiment of soldiers. Though their arrival causes such a stir in Meryton, *Pride and Prejudice* gives little sense of a country at war with revolutionary France. The 'restoration of peace' (p. 366) mentioned in the final chapter probably refers to one of the short intervals in the European war, which had seen Britain cut off from Europe. From 1804 Martello towers (some still standing) were built along the south and east coasts as defence against possible invasion by Napoleon.

SOCIAL CHANGE

War with France had dampened revolutionary idealism in Britain. But British society was in the midst of various and far-reaching change: a centuries-old agricultural economy was being replaced by city-based industry. Especially in the north of England (which Austen never visited), factories with water- and steam-powered machinery were taking over from domestic production. Fortunes were being made in textiles, iron and steel, mining and pottery; and industry was creating a new urban working class.

In religion, John Wesley's Methodists finally broke with the Church of England in 1795, four years after their founder's death. At their huge open-air evangelical meetings they emphasised the urgency of developing a personal relationship with God, simple worship, concern for the poor, and individual salvation.

Pride and Prejudice does not focus on these changes, but they do underlie some of the novel's premises. Lady Catherine's and Darcy's snobbery is not a sign of their confidence, and might be seen as a last effort by the old land-owning class to protect their rights and interests. The sneering attitude of Caroline Bingley to 'trade' – though we are told this is how her father made money in the north of England – indicates a nervousness about class boundaries that is a symptom of the social changes under way. Darcy's friendship with Bingley is an alliance of old gentry with the new would-be gentry; intermarriage would seal the pact.

THE CHURCH

Mr Collins is a **caricature** of an English clergyman. His 'living' is in the control of land-owners like Darcy and Lady Catherine. Mr Collins seems wholly insensitive to any spiritual aspect in his role. We hear nothing of his work in the parish. Like Elizabeth, the reader is shocked that Wickham could contemplate taking up his living in the Church. We can see Austen's portrayal of Mr Collins as an implicit criticism of a religious institution where men like him could easily find a career.

CRITICAL VIEWPOINT A04

Do you think Austen's novels emphasise social mobility or stasis? Is her society in a state of alteration, or complacently unchanging?

LITERARY BACKGROUND

AUSTEN'S OTHER WORKS

CHECK THE BOOK A03

What points of comparison and contrast can you identify between *Pride and Prejudice* and some of the modern texts you have been studying? Think about subject matter, language and form, for example.

Austen's juvenilia were skits and **satires** for the amusement of her family. Her first published novel, *Sense and Sensibility*, was a re-working of an earlier **epistolary** draft called *Elinor and Marianne*. *Northanger Abbey* is a spirited parody of the **Gothic** novel. *Mansfield Park* is a strange and somewhat moralistic book, quite different in tone from the early works, an attempt to write about a weak and unattractive but morally good heroine, Fanny Price. In *Emma* Austen describes the matchmaking and misapprehensions of a wealthy, clever but slightly spoilt young woman, and how she eventually achieves greater wisdom. *Persuasion* concerns the protracted courtship of a naval officer and the gentle, intelligent Anne Elliot, who is unloved by her snobbish father and sister. It is more gently concerned with the evaluation and description of feeling than the early novels. All these novels conclude with at least one marriage.

INFLUENCES ON AUSTEN

The first influences on Jane Austen's prose **style** would have been the Bible and the Book of Common Prayer. She read many books in her father's library, which was well stocked with classical authors. In its balanced style, in the satire of its **caricatures**, and in its moral concerns, *Pride and Prejudice* has many affinities with eighteenth-century literature, which valued moderation, order, common sense and reason, and liked to laugh at the folly of those who did not aspire to these values.

JOHNSON, RICHARDSON AND FIELDING

CONTEXT A04

The principal male novelist of Austen's time, Sir Walter Scott (1771–1832), had yet to publish: his first novel, *Waverley*, came out anonymously in 1814, a year after *Pride and Prejudice*.

Austen seems to have particularly admired Dr Johnson (1709–84), and the novels of Samuel Richardson (1689–1761). In *Pamela* (1740) and *Clarissa* (1748) Richardson portrayed through their letters the anguish of distressed females. *Sir Charles Grandison* (1754) achieved a new depth and subtlety in **characterisation**. Such works provide models for Austen's interest in the minds and feelings of her characters.

She also read *Tom Jones* (1749) by Henry Fielding (1707–54). Wickham's story of ill treatment by Darcy could be seen to echo the **plot** of *Tom Jones*, in which the hero Jones is ousted from the affections of Squire Allworthy by the villainous Blifil.

POETRY AND FEELING

CONTEXT A04

Aspiring women authors saw writing as a means of supporting themselves. Anne Radcliffe (1764–1823), for example, was paid £500 for the first publication of *The Mysteries of Udolpho* (1794), and £800 for *The Italian* (1797), both Gothic novels. Other women novelists of the time include Charlotte Smith (1749–1806), Fanny Burney (1752–1840) and Maria Edgeworth (1767–1849). Their novels centre on provincial and domestic life.

Austen read the works of poets such as George Crabbe (1754–1832), Sir Walter Scott (1771–1832), Lord Byron (1788–1824) and Robert Burns (1759–96). From them she would have learned the centrality of feeling in literature, and seen new ways of expressing it in language (this influence is observable in *Persuasion*). However, in her early novels she is more apt to mock the new focus on 'sensibility'. The variety of her novels shows a determined interest in developing the form of the novel, and a desire to experiment with new techniques and subject matter.

THE STATUS OF NOVELS

Notwithstanding the range of eighteenth-century fiction, the novel was still perceived as a relatively new and suspect form in the early nineteenth century. People like Mr Collins did not regard it as serious literature, unlike for example sermons, essays or poetry. The development of lending libraries in the mid-eighteenth century (there is one in Meryton) made novels widely available, and new kinds of novel were written to cater for this taste.

CRITICAL DEBATES

EARLY CRITICAL RECEPTION

Pride and Prejudice is presumed to have sold quite well: selling for eighteen shillings (about 90 pence) for the three volumes. The first edition of 1813 was followed by a second edition in the same year, and a third in 1817. However, it is not known how many copies were printed. Advertised as being 'by the Author of *Sense and Sensibility'*, which had itself been published as 'a New Novel by a Lady', Austen's anonymous work received considerable praise. An 1813 review said that *Pride and Prejudice* 'rises very superior to any novel we have lately met with in the delineation of domestic scenes'. Early criticism of Austen is brought together in *Jane Austen: The Critical Heritage* (1968).

VICTORIAN VIEWS

Charlotte Brontë thought Austen 'incomplete': 'the Passions are perfectly unknown to her', she wrote in 1850. In partial agreement with this kind of view, the influential critic George Henry Lewes wrote an article on 'The Novels of Jane Austen' in *Blackwood's Magazine* in 1859. He comments on her continued readership and survival after more popular novelists such as Maria Edgeworth had gone out of fashion. He admired in her 'the economy of art' without 'superfluous elements'.

The publication of *A Memoir of Jane Austen* by her nephew Edward Austen-Leigh in 1870 suddenly led to a burst of interest in both Jane Austen's life, which was previously unknown, and her novels. Unfortunately it led to the sentimentalisation of Austen, who was remodelled to fit some Victorian tastes, as a polite spinster genius. Out of this biographical approach grew the Janeites, fanatical admirers obsessed with every detail of the books and the author's life, and who often neglected to appreciate her intelligence as a novelist. Henry James called their effusions 'pleasant twaddle', but because the Janeites polarised opinion, the critical understanding of Austen became distorted. Many studies of her were written and some of a high quality, but the cult of Jane was overwhelmingly powerful at that time.

> **CHECK THE BOOK** A04
>
> There is an interesting chapter on the low status of the novel and the guilt that nineteenth-century novel readers sometimes felt in Kathleen Tillotson's *Novels of the Eighteen-Forties* (1954).

> **CONTEXT** A04
>
> There are several websites that continue the 'Janeite' tradition and contain an enormous quantity of helpful and enjoyable material such as frequently asked questions, lists of sequels and 'missing scenes' of the novels. Try searching for key words from an essay title.

TWENTIETH-CENTURY VIEWS

Eventually the publication of a serious academic study, *Jane Austen and her Art* (1939) by Mary Lascelles, put Austen criticism on a new professional footing. Lascelles countered Henry James's view that Austen was merely 'instinctive and charming' by analysing the artfulness of her composition.

In the university curriculum Austen quickly gained a remarkable ascendancy. Two influential works placed her centrally in the **canon** of great novelists. F. R. Leavis's *The Great Tradition* (1947) famously argued that Austen was no less than 'the inaugurator of the great tradition of the English novel'. Ian Watt's *The Rise of the Novel* (1957) saw her as the 'final logic' of the eighteenth-century novel.

THE NEW CRITICISM

CHECK THE BOOK A03

Two great studies of the novel from the 1960s grew out of the precepts of the New Criticism, but moved towards a more wide-ranging and theoretical understanding of fictional writing. They were *The Rhetoric of Fiction* (1961) by Wayne C. Booth and *Language of Fiction* (1966) by David Lodge.

The critical movement called New Criticism originated in the 1930s and 1940s in the USA, but dominated the academic study of literature there and in Britain from the 1950s until the 1970s. F. R. Leavis took many of his assumptions from the New Critics. They based their methods on the study of lyric poetry. Anxious to escape from the narrow biographical or amateur historical approaches, they isolated the literary text from its surrounding context of history and politics, and contemplated its design and structure for its own sake. Close reading of individual, autonomous texts dominated teaching and scholarship. The observation of linguistic effects, such as ambiguity, **irony**, **paradox**, image and symbol, came to be the sole task of the reader. There are many such studies, and many of them present interesting and subtle views of Austen's novels. Among the best is Barbara Hardy's *A Reading of Jane Austen* (1975).

One particular study of Austen's *Mansfield Park*, an essay by the American liberal critic Lionel Trilling in *The Opposing Self* (1955), deserves special mention because it sets an agenda for the examination of all her novels, including *Pride and Prejudice*. His high claims for Austen show the internal, private nature of the reading process, and its application to the self.

CONTEMPORARY APPROACHES

The belief that values and ideas and behaviour are universal has now given way to a different set of premises. 'Value' itself is now regarded as the construction of particular cultures. There is no **canon** of great writing, no 'great tradition': texts are classified as 'great' for particular reasons at particular times. The so-called 'classics' of English literature were put on a pedestal to support the cultural *status quo*, forcing out texts that were subversive and radical, and that challenged the dominant political and social elitism.

From the 1980s till the present, politics and history have been at the forefront of critical study. All language is deemed to be political, as it shapes the way in which we perceive the world. The study of Jane Austen's writing continues, and it has still proved available to widely divergent views.

CHECK THE BOOK A03

Marxist interpretations of key novels can be found in Arnold Kettle's *Introduction to the English Novel* (1951–2).

HISTORICIST CRITICISM

Historicist critics adopt many different approaches, with the common aim of placing a text or a writer more clearly and exactly within their original context, political or cultural. A Marxist analysis of Jane Austen, for example, would seek to find evidence of Austen's attitude to the growth of the working classes, to class divisions, the role of servants and the exercise of privilege.

- One very influential and groundbreaking study placed Austen in relation to the political and ideological arguments of her time. This was Marilyn Butler's *Jane Austen and the War of Ideas* (1990). Austen's novels are examined for their engagement in the debates that raged between the Jacobins and the anti-Jacobins, the supporters and the opponents of French revolutionary ideas. According to this study, Austen was partisan and she was conservative. Her heroines willingly adopt traditional subservient female roles. In this Austen is contrasted with Maria Edgeworth, whose novels were more challengingly radical.

- A more specialised and narrow study illustrating a historicist method is *Jane Austen and the Body* (1992) by John Wiltshire. This examines eighteenth-century and present-day ideas of illness and in the light of these examines references in Austen's novels to illness, blushing, 'nerves' and sensibility. These prove to be remarkably frequent in her work, though there is no separate examination of *Pride and Prejudice*.

FEMINIST CRITICISM

Feminist criticism examines the ways in which women (and men) are portrayed in novels, and considers the role of language and literature in relation to a culture and society which, most certainly in the time of Austen, and to a considerable extent nowadays, are dominated by men. It discovers groups of women writers, and female ways of writing, which have been ignored by the canon, and aims to re-assess the role of the woman writer in history.

"Had this offer of marriage you have refused?"
Chap. XX

- Judgement has not stabilised with regard to Austen. Some feminist readers, such as Marilyn Butler (whose study pre-dated the burgeoning of feminist writing), see her as the purveyor of feeble female acquiescence to the patriarchy. Others regard her as a subversive force for the good, mocking men and paying proper attention to the values of the female worlds that she describes.

- Julia Prewitt Brown's *Jane Austen's Novels* (1979) explores her writing in relation to the cult of the family in the early nineteenth century, and shows how the values of womanhood and domesticity were dignified, strengthened and idealised by this.

- Sandra M. Gilbert and Susan Gubar's *The Madwoman in the Attic: The Woman Writer and the Nineteenth-century Literary Imagination* (1979) surveys women's writing in the light of their exclusion from the male-dominated canon of literary greatness. Women writers have to find covert ways of subverting male culture, and Austen illustrates this in representations of female friendship, neurotic older women and weak fathers.

- Two other works continue the examination of Austen's novels in relation to her contemporary culture. In *Jane Austen: Feminism and Fiction* (1983) Margaret Kirkham examines the contemporary feminist controversies at the end of the eighteenth century. She finds that Austen implicitly espoused feminist views in her beliefs that women share the same moral nature and are as wholly responsible for their moral conduct as men.

- In *The Proper Lady and the Woman Writer* by Mary Poovey (1984), Austen's ideas of female propriety are compared to those of Mary Shelley and Mary Wollstonecraft.

TWENTY-FIRST-CENTURY CRITICISM

Various recent books continue to add to the variety of contemporary approaches. D. A. Millar's *Jane Austen, or the Secret of Style* (2003) argues that the anonymity and apparent universality of the **narrator** in the novels is a device borne of a reaction to the local details of her spinsterhood. There are, he observes, no successful unmarried women or female authors in the novels, no representations of anyone like Jane Austen herself. The narrator's stance represents a denial of Austen's self.

Others examine the Austen industry in its various different manifestations. In *Jane Austen on Film and Television: A Critical Study of the Adaptations* (2002), Sue Parrill explores the various ways in which Austen's novels have been transformed so as to conform to modern tastes, offering analysis of individual adaptations. In *Recreating Jane Austen* (2001), a more theoretical approach is taken by John Wiltshire who pays particular attention to *Pride and Prejudice* in his examination of Austen's special place in the present-day cultural imagination.

CHECK THE BOOK A04

Bridget Jones' Diary (1997) by Helen Fielding, also a successful film, offers a strange and parodic comment on *Pride and Prejudice*. Its action roughly echoes the plot – but in the midst of a quite different moral world.

CONTEXT A03

Due in no small part to the bicentenary of the publication of *Pride and Prejudice* in 2013, there continues to be great interest in Austen's life and work and a large readership for books about her work as well as the novels themselves. You can search for recent books on Jane Austen online.

CHECK THE BOOK A04

Matters of fact in Jane Austen: History, Location and Celebrity by Janine Barchas (2012) examines how precise Austen was regarding the historical and political figures and locations that feature in her novels.

ASSESSMENT FOCUS

WHAT ARE YOU BEING ASKED TO FOCUS ON?

The questions or tasks you are set will be based around the four **Assessment Objectives**, **AO1** to **AO4**.

You may get more marks for certain **AOs** than others depending on which unit you're working on. Check with your teacher if you are unsure.

WHAT DO THESE AOs ACTUALLY MEAN?

	ASSESSMENT OBJECTIVES	MEANING?
AO1	Articulate creative, informed and relevant responses to literary texts, using appropriate terminology and concepts, and coherent, accurate written expression.	You write about texts in accurate, clear and precise ways so that what you have to say is clear to the marker. You use literary terms (e.g. **bathos**) or refer to concepts (e.g. **intertextuality**) in relevant places.
AO2	Demonstrate detailed critical understanding in analysing the ways in which structure, form and language shape meanings in literary texts.	You show that you understand the specific techniques and methods used by the writer(s) to create the text (e.g. **characterisation**, **irony**, etc.). You can explain clearly how these methods affect the meaning.
AO3	Explore connections and comparisons between different literary texts, informed by interpretations of other readers.	You are able to see relevant links between different texts. You are able to comment on how others (such as critics) view the text.
AO4	Demonstrate understanding of the significance and influence of the contexts in which literary texts are written and received.	You can explain how social, historical, political or personal backgrounds to the texts affected the writer and how the texts were read when they were first published and at different times since.

WHAT DOES THIS MEAN FOR YOUR REVISION?

Depending on the course you are following, you could be asked to:

- Respond to a general question about the text as a whole. For example:

Explore the ways Austen uses comedy and caricature in *Pride and Prejudice*.

- Write about an aspect of *Pride and Prejudice* which is also a feature of other texts you are studying. These questions may take the form of a challenging statement or quotation which you are invited to discuss. For example:

'The novel is perfectly suited to depicting human nature in all its complexity.' How far do you agree with this view?

- Or you may have to focus on the particular similarities, links, contrasts and differences between this text and others. For example:

Compare the author's treatment of marriage in *Pride and Prejudice* and in other text(s) you are studying.

EXAMINER'S TIP

Make sure you know how many marks are available for each **AO** in the task you are set. This can help to divide up your time or decide how much attention to give each aspect.

TARGETING A HIGH GRADE

It is very important to understand the progression from a lower grade to a high grade. In all cases, it is not enough simply to mention some key points and references – instead, you should explore them in depth, drawing out what is interesting and relevant to the question or issue.

TYPICAL C GRADE FEATURES

	FEATURES	EXAMPLES
A01	You use critical vocabulary accurately, and your arguments make sense, are relevant and focus on the task. You show detailed knowledge of the text.	The narrator's opening remark and the dialogue between Mr and Mrs Bennet indicate that marriage will be a central theme of this novel.
A02	You can say how some specific aspects of form, structure and language shape meanings.	Letters are used throughout the novel. Austen adopts the writing style of many different characters in the form of letters, helping the reader to see events from a range of perspectives.
A03	You consider, in detail, the connections between texts, and also how interpretations of texts differ, with some relevant supporting references.	Some modern critics have defended the character of Mrs Bennet. They have argued that her obsession with getting her daughters married is simply a reflection of the times in which the novel is set. Her anxiety about the entailment could be likened to the Dashwoods feeling displaced from their own home in Austen's "Sense and Sensibility".
A04	You can write about a range of contextual factors and make some specific and detailed links between these and the task or text.	Readers at the time would have known that a family like the Bennets would have employed a number of staff. A household like Pemberley, however, would have had a bigger staff, in keeping with the Darcy family's wealth and status. Indeed, at Pemberley, Elizabeth considers 'how many people's happiness were in his guardianship' (p. 240), meaning Darcy's sister, his staff and also his tenants.

TYPICAL FEATURES OF AN A OR A* RESPONSE

	FEATURES	EXAMPLES
A01	You use appropriate critical vocabulary, technical terms and a clear, fluent style. Your arguments are well structured, coherent and always relevant, with a sharp focus on task.	The narrator opens the novel with a sentence that begins like a witty and philosophical aphorism – 'It is a truth universally acknowledged …' – but whose subject matter could be seen as rather mundane by comparison. The effect is to establish a gently ironic narrative voice, alive to the scope for social satire as well as for romantic storytelling in this tale about the marriage prospects of the Bennet daughters. It follows then that most of the opening chapter is domestic dialogue with little authorial comment to interrupt it.
A02	You explore and analyse key aspects of form, structure and language, and evaluate perceptively how they shape meanings.	Austen cleverly uses letters to advance the plot and to reveal much about characters' temperament as well as their motivations; Mr Bennet is a poor letter-writer, Lydia a writer only of short missives, somewhat lacking in insight or reflection. Meanwhile, Darcy – whose letter-writing style was gently mocked earlier in the novel for his tendency to 'study too much for words of four syllables' (p. 47) – writes a frank and intense letter to Elizabeth which is the catalyst for her reassessment of, and change of heart towards, both Wickham and Darcy himself.
A03	You show a detailed and perceptive understanding of issues raised through connections between texts and can consider different interpretations with a sharp evaluation of their strengths and weaknesses. You have a range of excellent supporting references.	There is a striking contrast between our constant awareness of family and society in Austen's novels and the isolation of the abandoned or spurned lover in Tennyson's "Mariana", for example. Austen's depiction of Jane's stoical but pained reaction to Bingley's departure and apparent lack of interest in her is affecting but Jane's reactions share the page with those of other characters, not least Mrs Bennet's tactless remarks. Thus the impact of personal sadness is softened for the reader by social comedy. By contrast, Mariana's suffering is described repeatedly, every description of Mariana's surroundings being a reflection of the hopelessness with which she views her situation.
A04	You show a deep, detailed and relevant understanding(s) of how contextual factors link to the text or task.	England was at war with France throughout much of Austen's adult life and many towns in the south of England at this time would, like Meryton, have witnessed the arrival and departure of militia regiments. While the wars themselves are absent from the novel, the presence of the regiment in Meryton is felt keenly by Lydia and Kitty who make much of the slightest rumour or sighting of uniformed officers. The novel's scope does not extend to broader political or military concerns, but, by entering Meryton society, the militia – and Wickham in particular – become a key concern for the novel and many of its characters.

HOW TO WRITE HIGH-QUALITY RESPONSES

The quality of your writing – how you express your ideas – is vital for getting a higher grade, and **AO1** and **AO2** are specifically about **how** you respond.

FIVE KEY AREAS

The quality of your responses can be broken down into **five** key areas.

1. THE STRUCTURE OF YOUR ANSWER/ESSAY

- First, get **straight to the point in your opening paragraph.** Use a sharp, direct first sentence that deals with a key aspect and then follows up with evidence or a detailed reference.
- **Put forward an argument or point of view** (you won't **always** be able to challenge or take issue with the essay question, but generally, where you can, you are more likely to write in an interesting way).
- **Signpost your ideas** with connectives and references, which help the essay flow.
- **Don't repeat points already made**, not even in the conclusion, unless you have something new to say that adds a further dimension.

TARGETING A HIGH GRADE

Here's an example of an opening paragraph that gets straight to the point, addressing the question:

'Pride and Prejudice is centrally concerned with personal happiness and the grounds on which it might be achieved.' (Vivien Jones) How do you respond to this viewpoint?

"Pride and Prejudice" is indeed concerned with the achievement of personal happiness but not at any cost. When Lydia writes to Elizabeth to wish her 'joy' and tell her that if she loves Darcy 'half as well as I do my dear Wickham, you must be very happy' (p. 365), the reader is reminded that happiness represents different Immediate focus on task and key words with example from text

things for different characters. For Charlotte Lucas, the security a marriage brings matters more than marital joy although Charlotte does appear to achieve a degree of contentment by marrying Mr Collins. But it is Elizabeth's marriage to Darcy – the novel's central narrative – that is portrayed most convincingly by Austen as combining personal attraction and compatibility of character, along with everything a good marriage represents in terms of financial security, social standing and inheritance.

2. USE OF TITLES, NAMES, ETC.

This is a simple, but important, tip to stay on the right side of the examiners.

- Make sure that you spell correctly the titles of the texts, chapters, name of authors and so on. Present them correctly, too, with double quotation marks and capitals as appropriate. For example, '*In Volume One, Chapter I (Chapter 1) of "Pride and Prejudice" …*'.
- Use the **full title**, unless there is a good reason not to (e.g. it's very long).
- Use the terms 'novel' or 'text' rather than ' book' or 'story'. If you use the word 'story', the examiner may think you mean the plot/action rather than the 'text' as a whole.

3. EFFECTIVE QUOTATIONS

Do not 'bolt on' quotations to the points you make. You will get some marks for including them, but examiners will not find your writing very fluent.

The best quotations are:

- Relevant
- Not too long
- Integrated into your argument/sentence.

TARGETING A HIGH GRADE   A01

Here is an example of quotations successfully embedded in a sentence:

Mr Collins believes that Elizabeth's refusal of him is due only to her 'true delicacy' (p. 105) and 'bashful modesty' (p. 108). This stereotypical view of femininity is at odds with the reader's view of Elizabeth as an intelligent and spirited character who is not afraid to speak her mind.

Remember – quotations can also be a well-selected set of three or four single words or phrases embedded in a sentence to build a picture or explanation. Or they can be longer ones that are explored and picked apart.

4. TECHNIQUES AND TERMINOLOGY

By all means mention literary terms, techniques, conventions or people (for example, '**omniscient narrator**' or '**epistolary novel**' or 'Mary Wollstonecraft') **but** make sure that you:

- Understand what they mean or who they are
- Are able to link them to what you're saying
- Spell them correctly.

5. GENERAL WRITING SKILLS

Try to write in a way that sounds professional and uses standard English. This does not mean that your writing will lack personality – just that it will be authoritative.

- Avoid colloquial or everyday expressions such as 'got', 'alright', 'ok' and so on.
- Use terms such as 'convey', 'suggest', 'imply', 'infer' to explain the writer's methods.
- Refer to 'we' when discussing the audience/reader.
- Avoid assertions and generalisations; don't just state a general point of view ('Elizabeth refuses Mr Collins's proposal because he is boring'), but analyse closely, with clear evidence and textual detail.

TARGETING A HIGH GRADE   A01

Note the professional approach in this example:

Austen's presentation of Mr Collins allows the reader to see that he is no match for Elizabeth and makes her refusal of him seem a foregone conclusion. Both Elizabeth and her father conjure up an accurate and amusing image of Mr Collins on the basis of his letter announcing his impending arrival: 'Can he be a sensible man, sir?' (p. 63). Meanwhile his attempts at 'gallantry' (p. 63) and 'solemnity' (p. 67) are, ironically, taken seriously by Mrs Bennet and Mary, whose judgement we are likely to question. Given Mr Collins's long-windedness, pomposity and obsequious praise for Lady Catherine, it is no surprise that Mr Bennet finds his guest 'absurd' (p. 67) nor that Mr Collins's proposal causes in Elizabeth feelings 'which were divided between distress and diversion' (p. 103). Occasional passages of authorial intervention, in which we learn more about Mr Collins's upbringing and education, do little to overturn our first impressions of the self-important clergyman.

GRADE BOOSTER A02

It is important to remember that *Pride and Prejudice* is a text created by Austen. Thinking about the voices Austen creates through language and plotting will alert you not only to her methods as an author, but also to her intentions, i.e. the effect she seeks to create.

CLOSE READING OF SPECIFIC EXTRACTS

Reading and responding to a specific extract or section of the text is an essential part of your study of *Pride and Prejudice* You will be expected to select appropriate information, draw conclusions and make interpretations. When it comes to your exam, you may be asked to focus on a specific part of the text you are studying. For example:

> How does Austen tell the story in Volume Three, Chapter I (Chapter 43)?

It is important that, from your study, you are familiar with:

- **Where** and **when** this passage/chapter occurs **in the text** (is it an ending of a sequence of events or the actual end of a chapter or key section? Where does it happen in 'real time'?)
- What is **significant** about the extract in terms of **the writer's methods (AO2)** (for example, whose voice is it related through? What events or characters are revealed in what order? How is it structured, etc?)

WRITING AN EXAM RESPONSE

You must comment on the **writer's methods** specifically (*how* Austen does it):

DO	DON'T
• Consider Austen's narrative style and structures, for example the use of **dialogue** and **free indirect speech** throughout the chapter.	• Just re-tell the story/plot
• Explore Austen's use of language, for example how she describes the grounds, the house and its contents and Mrs Reynolds the housekeeper.	• Just write about who the characters are and what they do
• Think about the importance of setting and how Austen uses different types of homes throughout the novel to symbolise characters' values and aspirations.	• State what the themes are unless linked to the writer's methods
• Focus on form, for example, Austen's placement of passages of a more judgemental style of narration.	• 'Micro-analyse' – in other words, don't write extensively on just one single word or a particular type of punctuation. This may look impressive, but you need to be sensible about how much real impact those choices the writer makes may have.

There are **two** key things you should do when writing about an extract:

- Focus immediately on a specific aspect
- Develop your points with detail

For example, in your first paragraph immediately focus on a key aspect of the writer's methods. Don't waste time with general waffle or plot summary.

> *In the opening to this extract, Austen uses description to …*

In your second paragraph introduce further ideas or develop your first point in more detail.

> *Once inside the house, Austen continues to blend description with Elizabeth's perspective on what she sees.*

In further paragraphs you should aim to cover new methods used by the writer and make links between and across the methods. As a whole, your essay should work towards a clear, precise conclusion that directly answers the question.

RESPONDING TO A GENERAL QUESTION ABOUT THE WHOLE TEXT

> **Explore the role and status of women in society as presented by Austen in**
> *Pride and Prejudice.*

Alternatively, you may also be asked to write about a specific aspect of *Pride and Prejudice* – but as it relates to the **whole text**. For example:

This means you should:

- Focus on *both* **women's role** *and* **women's status**.
- **Explain their 'presentation'** – *how* Austen presents these issues through the novel's plot, characters and treatment of themes such as love, marriage and money.
- Look at aspects of the **whole novel**, not just one part of it.

STRUCTURING YOUR RESPONSE

You need a clear, logical plan, as for all tasks that you do. It is impossible to write about every section or part of the text, so you will need to:

- Quickly note 5–6 key points or aspects to build your essay around, e.g.

Point a *Sexual propriety is considered to be of the utmost importance for women, and Lydia would have brought even more disgrace to her family had marriage to Wickham not been negotiated.*

Point b *The novel centres on the matter of finding eligible husbands for daughters and the financial security that results from a good match.*

Point c *The prospect of not marrying is not presented particularly attractively. Charlotte Lucas takes trouble to win her husband despite his shortcomings, and Mary's life at home with her parents sounds claustrophobic and leaves her less time for her interests than she previously had.*

Point d *The novel features some discussion of suitable pastimes for a woman which are largely domestic and are more about presenting a particular image of femininity to onlookers than they are about physical, intellectual or creative achievement.*

Point e *A young woman's appearance is of great importance. Whereas Jane and Elizabeth are described flatteringly, some characters such as Charlotte are considered 'plain'.*

- Then decide the most effective or logical order. For example, **point b**, then **c, d, a, e**, etc.

You could begin with your key or main idea, with supporting evidence/references, followed by your further points (perhaps two paragraphs for each). For example:

Paragraph 1: first key point: *In "Pride and Prejudice", it is made clear from the opening sentence that the role of 'wife' is of central importance in the society that Austen depicts.*

Paragraph 2: expand out, link into other areas: *It is also clear, particularly from Elizabeth's first visit to Pemberley, but also from the pressure she was under to accept Mr Collins's hand in marriage because of the entailment, that a woman's social status can be dramatically changed by marriage.*

Paragraph 3: change direction, introduce new aspect/point: *Conversely, the prospect of not marrying is not presented as an enviable outcome for women. Charlotte Lucas takes trouble to win her husband, despite his shortcomings, for the status and security the role of wife provides. Meanwhile, Austen describes Mary's life as a spinster at home with her parents in a rather claustrophobic fashion. Mary is left with less time for her interests than she previously had.* And so on.

- For your **conclusion**, use a compelling way to finish, perhaps repeating some or all of the key words from the question. For example:

End with your final point, but **add a last clause** which makes it clear what you think is key to the question: e.g. *A young woman's appearance is shown to be of great importance since the extent to which she is admired by potential suitors is an indicator of her future success in winning the heart of an eligible man. Time and again, Austen presents women as dependent on the institution of marriage in order to enhance their role and status in society.*

EXAMINER'S TIP ✓

You may be asked to discuss other texts you have studied as well as *Pride and Prejudice* as part of your response. Once you have completed your response on the novel you could move on to discuss the same issues in your other text(s). Begin with a simple linking phrase or sentence to launch straight into your first point about your next text, such as: *'The same idea/issue is explored in quite a different way in [name of text] … Here …'*

EXAMINER'S TIP ✓

Alternatively, you could end with a **new quotation** or an **aspect that's slightly different from** your main point: *However, it remains the case for all of the sisters, whatever their attitude and temperament, that their role and status are governed by patriarchal values, and that marriage – and presumably motherhood – are their virtually inevitable destinies.*

QUESTIONS WITH STATEMENTS, QUOTATIONS OR VIEWPOINTS

One type of question you may come across includes a statement, quotation or viewpoint from another reader.

These questions ask you to respond to, or argue for/against, a specific point of view or critical interpretation.

For *Pride and Prejudice* these questions will typically be like this:

- Discuss the view that Austen's depiction of family life in *Pride and Prejudice* is more comic than credible.
- How far do you agree with the idea that Austen gives *Pride and Prejudice* a fairy-tale ending?
- 'Mrs Bennet dominates the book from its opening sentence.' (Claire Tomalin) To what extent do you agree with this statement?

The key thing to remember is that you are being asked to **respond to a critical interpretation** of the text – in other words, to come up with **your own** 'take' on the idea or viewpoint in the task.

KEY SKILLS REQUIRED

The table below provides help and advice on answering this type of question:

- To what extent do you agree that 'there seems no defect in the portrait' of Elizabeth Bennet? (Unsigned notice, *British Critic*, 1813)

SKILL	MEANS?	HOW DO I ACHIEVE THIS?
Consider different interpretations	There will be more than one way of looking at the given question. For example, it could be interpreted as meaning that Elizabeth is an idealised heroine with few if any flaws, or alternatively that it is the realism and humanity of Austen's portrayal of Elizabeth that is 'without defect'.	• Show you have considered these different interpretations in your answer. For example: *Elizabeth Bennet is presented by Austen to be a very assured, intelligent, witty and handsome young woman. However, she is not presented as a flawless or idealised character and is perhaps most attractive to readers when she is at her most unconventional and outspoken. It could be argued that it is the honesty with which she confronts her own errors of judgement that makes Elizabeth Bennet so sympathetic as a character. While some critics have criticised the speed of Darcy's transformation from gruffness and snobbery to perceptiveness and humility, Elizabeth's development has been more widely praised for its credibility. In other words, it is in Elizabeth's all too human 'defects' that the success of Austen's characterisation lies.*
Write with a clear, personal voice	Your own 'take' on the question is made obvious to the marker. You are not just repeating other people's ideas, but offering what **you** think.	• Although you may mention different perspectives on the task, you settle on your own view. • Use language that shows careful, but confident, consideration. For example: *Although it has been said that … I feel that …*
Construct a coherent argument	The examiner or marker can follow your train of thought so that your own viewpoint is clear to him or her.	• Write in clear paragraphs that deal logically with different aspects of the question. • Support what you say with well-selected and relevant evidence. • Use a range of connectives to help 'signpost' your argument. For example: *Expanding upon … However, such a view fails to take account of … Notwithstanding the power of this argument, it is important to …*

ANSWERING A 'VIEWPOINT' QUESTION

Here is an example of a typical question on *Pride and Prejudice*:

> Discuss the view that 'Austen's novels are fables which act out traditional concepts of the qualities and the role of the gentry'. (Marilyn Butler, 1981)

STAGE 1: DECODE THE QUESTION

Underline/highlight the **key words**, and make sure you understand what the statement, quotation or viewpoint is saying. In this case:

Key words = Discuss/fables/traditional/gentry

The viewpoint/idea expressed is = Austen's storytelling deliberately sets out to reinforce traditional attitudes about the qualities of the landed upper classes and their role in society.

STAGE 2: DECIDE WHAT YOUR VIEWPOINT IS

Examiners have stated that they tend to reward a strong view which is clearly put. Think about the question – can you take issue with it? Disagreeing strongly can lead to higher marks, provided you have **genuine evidence** to support your point of view. Don't disagree just for the sake of it.

STAGE 3: DECIDE HOW TO STRUCTURE YOUR ANSWER

Pick out the key points you wish to make, and decide on the order in which you will present them. Keep this basic plan to hand while you write your response.

STAGE 4: WRITE YOUR RESPONSE

You could start by expanding on the statement or viewpoint expressed in the question.

- For example, in **paragraph 1**:

  It is certainly true that Jane Austen predominantly shows us the lives of the landed gentry in "Pride and Prejudice". It is relatively rare for household servants to be mentioned and named, let alone the lower classes living elsewhere in the vicinity. Indeed, not only are the landed gentry the only characters to whom Austen introduces us in any depth, but their concerns throughout the novel – chiefly marriage and inheritance – are also rather inward-looking.

This could help by setting up the various ideas you will choose to explore, argue for/ against, and so on. But do not just repeat what the question says or just say what you are going to do. Get straight to the point. For example:

  The marriages of both Jane and Elizabeth could be read as a fable in that their happy endings reward the many admirable qualities both the sisters and their suitors have been shown to possess over the course of the novel.

Then, proceed to set out the different arguments or critical perspectives, including your own. This might be done by dealing with specific aspects or elements of the novel, one by one. Consider giving 1–2 paragraphs to explore each aspect in turn. Discuss the strengths and weaknesses in each particular point of view. For example:

- **Paragraph 2**: first aspect:

  *To answer whether this interpretation is valid, we need to **first of all** look at …*

  It is clear from this *that … /a **strength** of this argument is*

  ***However**, I believe this suggests that …/a **weakness** in this argument is*

- **Paragraph 3**: a new focus or aspect:

  Turning our attention to the critical idea that *… it could be said that …*

- **Paragraphs 4, 5, etc., onwards**: develop the argument, building a convincing set of points:

  ***Furthermore**, if we look at …*

- **Last paragraph**: end with a clear statement of your view, without simply listing all the points you have made:

  To say that "Pride and Prejudice" acts out traditional views about the qualities and roles of the landed gentry is true to some extent but that does not mean that Austen presents the gentry uncritically …

EXAMINER'S TIP

You should comment concisely, professionally and thoughtfully and present a range of viewpoints. Try using modal verbs such as 'could', 'might', 'may' to clarify your own interpretation. For additional help on **Using critical interpretations and perspectives,** see pages 114 and 115.

EXAMINER'S TIP

Note how the ideas are clearly signposted through a range of connectives and linking phrases, such as 'However' and 'Turning our attention to …'

COMPARING *PRIDE AND PREJUDICE* WITH OTHER TEXTS

As part of your assessment, you may have to compare *Pride and Prejudice* with, or link it to, other texts that you have studied. These may be other plays, novels or poetry. You may also have to link or draw in references from texts written by critics. For example:

Compare the presentation of reason and passion in *Pride and Prejudice* and other text(s) you have studied.

THE TASK

Your task is likely to be on a method, issue, viewpoint or key aspect that is common to *Pride and Prejudice* and the other text(s), so you will need to:

Evaluate the issue or statement and have an **open-minded approach**. The best answers suggest meaning**s** and interpretation**s** (plural):

- What do you understand by the question? Is this theme more important in one text than in another? Why? How?
- What are the different ways that this question or aspect can be read or viewed?
- Can you challenge the viewpoint, if there is one? If so, what evidence is there? How can you present it in a thoughtful, reflective way?

Express **original or creative approaches** fluently:

- This isn't about coming up with entirely new ideas, but you need to show that you're actively engaged with thinking about the question, not just reproducing random facts and information you have learned.
- **Synthesise** your ideas – pull ideas and points together to create something fresh.
- This is a linking/comparison response, so ensure that you guide your reader through your ideas logically, clearly and with professional language.

Know **what to compare/contrast: form, structure** and **language** will **always** be central to your response, even where you also have to write about characters, contexts or culture.

- Think about standard versus more unconventional narration (for example, first or third person, **omniscient narration**, multiple narrators, **free indirect speech**, use of letters, **foreshadowing**, disrupted time, stream of consciousness).
- Consider different characteristic use of language: length of sentences, length of paragraphs; formal/informal style; balance of **dialogue** and narration; styles of dialogue and narration; use of descriptive and **metaphorical** language; the difference between forms, if appropriate, or the different ways two novels use the possibilities offered by the novel form.
- Look at a variety of **symbols, images, motifs** (how they represent the concerns of the author and/or the time when the text was written; what they are and how and where they appear; how they link to critical perspectives; their purposes, effects and impact on the novel).
- Consider aspects of genres (to what extent do Austen and the author(s) of the other work(s) conform to/challenge/subvert particular genres or styles of writing?).

WRITING YOUR RESPONSE

The depth and extent of your answer will depend on how much you have to write, but the key will be to **explore in detail**, and **link between ideas and texts**. Let's use this example:

> Compare the presentation of reason and passion in *Pride and Prejudice* and other text(s) you have studied.

INTRODUCTION TO YOUR RESPONSE

- Discuss what 'reason and passion' mean, and how well these concepts apply to your texts. You may wish to briefly draw on classical, everyday or literary definitions.

- Briefly comment on the **importance** of reason and passion in *Pride and Prejudice* and the other text(s).

- You could begin with a powerful quotation. For example:

> *'She had no difficulty in believing that neither her virtue nor her understanding would preserve her from falling an easy prey' (p. 266). In this quotation, we see Elizabeth assessing her sister Lydia's susceptibility to the charms of Wickham. She finds much of her sister's behaviour questionable, believing with little difficulty that Lydia has allowed her attraction to Wickham and romantic notions about his love for her to tempt her from more reasonable conduct …*

MAIN BODY OF YOUR RESPONSE

- **Point 1**: start with the themes of reason and passion in *Pride and Prejudice* and how they are presented. What is your view? Are the ways in which they are presented similar in the other text(s)? Are there any relevant critical viewpoints or contexts to consider?

- **Point 2**: now cover a new treatment or aspect through comparison or contrast of this theme in your other text(s). How is this treatment or aspect presented **differently or similarly** by the writer(s) in the language, form, structures used? Why was this done in this way? How does it reflect the writers' interests? What do the critics say? Are there contextual or cultural factors to consider?

- **Points 3, 4, 5, etc.**: address a range of other factors and aspects, for example the importance of reason and passion for male as well as female characters **either** within *Pride and Prejudice* **or** in both *Pride and Prejudice* and another text. In what different ways do you respond to these other characters – and why? For example:

> *The themes of instinctive passion and more considered reasonable conduct also apply to male characters within both novels. It transpires that Wickham, for all that he appears a gentleman, has a past in which he has been indulgent and wasteful, prioritising pleasure over propriety.*

CONCLUSION TO YOUR RESPONSE

- Synthesise elements of what you have said into a final paragraph that fluently, succinctly and inventively leaves the reader/examiner with the sense that you have engaged with this task and the texts. For example:

> *Both Austen and Fowles present the reader with complex characters in whom different ideas and influences sometimes compete for supremacy. In Austen's novel, the characters who are most easily led by their passions are not the novel's protagonists and we are invited to judge their conduct more than understand it. For Fowles, love, sex and passion are presented as more complex and mysterious in their own right, and through his use of multiple endings, the author does not allow the reader to feel confident about any particular outcome or secure in any moral judgement about what has occurred.*

EXAMINER'S TIP

Be creative with your conclusion! It's the last thing the examiner will read and your chance to make your mark.

USING CRITICAL INTERPRETATIONS AND PERSPECTIVES

THE 'MEANING' OF A TEXT

There are many viewpoints and perspectives on the 'meaning' of *Pride and Prejudice*, and examiners will be looking for evidence that you have considered a range of these. Broadly speaking, these different interpretations might relate to the following:

1. CHARACTER

What **sort/type** of person Elizabeth, Darcy or another character is:

- Is the character an 'archetype' (a specific type of character with common features)? For example, Wickham's womanising and debts have seen him described as a 'rake' or 'libertine'. To what extent does he match that description?

- Does the character personify, symbolise or represent a specific idea or trope? For example, to what extent do Darcy and Elizabeth represent the 'pride' and 'prejudice' of the novel's title? What are the potential limitations of viewing characters in this way?

- Is the character modern, universal, of his/her time, historically accurate, etc.? Can we draw parallels between the descriptions of how families like the Bingleys and the Lucases made their fortunes in 'trade' and any of our own attitudes today about social mobility and the nouveau riche?

2. IDEAS AND ISSUES

What the novel tells us about **particular ideas or issues** and how we can interpret these. For example:

- the importance of understanding a person's character as fully as possible
- the significance of marriage in financial and social terms
- family, class, wealth and status
- the prevailing views of the time about suitable activities for men and women to pursue

3. LINKS AND CONTEXTS

To what extent the novel **links with, follows or pre-echoes** other texts and/or ideas. For example:

- Its influence culturally, historically and socially (do we see echoes of the characters or genres in other texts?). To what extent were later novelists inspired by Austen's works? How would you assess the popularity and wider cultural impact of Austen's novels today?

- How did Austen's novels contribute to the development of the novel form? Which novels particularly inspired Austen? How did Austen respond in her novels to Romanticism, to the **Gothic**, to feminist writings of the time and to the novels of sensibility of the eighteenth century?

4. NARRATIVE STRUCTURE

How the novel is **constructed** and how Austen **makes** her narrative:

- Does it follow particular narrative conventions?
- What is the function of specific events, characters, plot devices, locations, etc. in relation to narrative?
- What are the specific moments of tension, conflict, crisis and denouement?

CRITICAL VIEWPOINT **A03**

'Here was an outspoken young woman, very often wrong in her judgements and behaviour, yet always captivating, brilliantly lively and wholly human, whether speaking for herself or presented through the eyes of others. With her sisterly love and loyalty, her teasing, her articulacy, her repartee, her "archness rising to the eye that makes one both love and fear her", Charlotte Grandison was surely an early inspiration for Elizabeth Bennet'. (Claire Tomalin writing about a character from Samuel Richardson's 1753 epistolary novel *The History of Sir Charles Grandison*)

5. READER RESPONSE

How the novel **works on a reader**, and whether this changes over time and in different contexts:

- How does Austen **position** the reader? Are we to empathise with, feel distance from, judge and/or evaluate the events and characters?

6. CRITICAL REACTION

And finally, how different readers view the novel: for example, different reviewers, critics and fans over time.

WRITING ABOUT CRITICAL PERSPECTIVES

The important thing to remember is that **you** are a critic too. Your job is to evaluate what a critic or school of criticism has said about the elements above, and arrive at your own conclusions.

In essence, you need to: **consider** the views of others, **synthesise** them, then decide on **your perspective**. For example:

EXPLAIN THE VIEWPOINTS:

Critical view A about passion in Jane Austen's novels

> *In the nineteenth century, Charlotte Brontë expressed a reservation about Austen's novels, writing that 'the Passions are perfectly unknown to her'.*

Critical view B about passion in Jane Austen's novels

> *Twentieth-century feminist critics Sandra Gilbert and Susan Gubar write that Austen makes fun of 'novelistic clichés' such as 'love at first sight' and 'the primacy of passion over all other emotions and/or duties'.*

THEN SYNTHESISE AND ADD YOUR PERSPECTIVE:

TARGETING A HIGH GRADE (A04)

Various commentators have suggested that Austen's concerns are more with matters of the mind than with those of the heart. Discussions and disagreements between potential suitors are often included in their entirety in "Pride and Prejudice" whereas declarations of love are perhaps more chastely depicted, for example when Bingley proposes to Jane. However, it could be argued that it is not that Austen deliberately averts her (and our) eyes from moments of passion in the novel but rather that she does not wish to fall into the romantic novelist's trap of portraying love as arising purely from passionate attraction.

In my opinion, Austen writes about passion in the way she does neither out of ignorance nor out of a desire to make fun of romantic clichés. We do see flickers of passion in the novel such as Elizabeth's attraction to Wickham, and Darcy and Elizabeth's tongue-tied embarrassment at Pemberley. Moreover, it would seem that a giddy passion is what has united Wickham and Lydia, not to mention Mr and Mrs Bennet – both marriages which are presented to us as cautionary tales. Austen is showing us that the consequences of passion alone are not necessarily happy, and that a more grounded understanding of, and esteem for, one's betrothed is a more important indicator of 'connubial felicity' in the future.

GRADE BOOSTER (A03)

Make sure you have thoroughly explored the different kinds of criticism written about *Pride and Prejudice*. Critical interpretations of novels can range from reviews and comments written about the text at the time that it was first published through to critical analysis by a modern critic or a reader writing today. Bear in mind that views of texts can change over time as values and experiences themselves change, and that criticism can be written for different purposes.

ANNOTATED SAMPLE ANSWERS

Below are extracts from two sample answers to the same question at different grades. Bear in mind that these are examples only, covering AO1, AO3 and AO4. You will need to check the type of question and the weightings given for the Assessment Objectives when writing your coursework essay or practising for your exam.

> Question: **It could be argued that true love triumphs in *Pride and Prejudice*. To what extent do you agree with this description of the novel?**

CANDIDATE 1

"Pride and Prejudice" famously opens with the line: 'It is a truth universally acknowledged, that a single man in possession of a good fortune, must be in want of a wife' (p. 5). The institution of marriage at the time Jane Austen was writing was a very important aim to aspire to. The novel's various romantic plots end in marriage so it would seem that true love does triumph.

AO4 — Relevant contextual point but is not expressed clearly. Needs to be developed further

Elizabeth and Darcy are interesting because they are opposed to each other as protagonist and antagonist throughout a large part of the book. At the Netherfield ball, Darcy says that it would be a 'punishment ... to stand up with' (p. 13) Elizabeth or any other woman there with whom he is not already acquainted. He is wealthy but generally considered to be proud and disagreeable. Later on, Elizabeth and the novel's readers begin to understand Darcy's character better but their first impressions are not positive. The lost earlier draft of "Pride and Prejudice" was called "First Impressions", which is an appropriate title given that it is Darcy and Elizabeth's false first impressions of each other that prevent them from seeing each other in a romantic light.

AO1 — Some use of critical vocabulary and literary terms

AO4 — Good use of background knowledge

Darcy begins to become attracted to Elizabeth, but when he first proposes to her and is refused, he describes his affections for her in a way she finds 'wounding' (p. 185). He emphasises their different social status and the fact that 'in vain' he has 'struggled' (p. 185) to reconcile his feelings with his better judgement and pride. Additionally, Elizabeth's view of Darcy has been prejudiced by Wickham's account of how he has treated him and ruined 'perhaps, for ever, the happiness of a most beloved sister' (p. 186). At this roughly halfway point in the novel, pride and prejudice are triumphing, not true love. Austen makes this clear by using words like 'deeply-rooted dislike' (p. 185) and 'contemptuously' (p. 187) to describe their feelings and way of speaking.

AO1 — Good use of embedded quotations in this paragraph

A03

Well focused on question but other viewpoints on the statement are not explored

True love is seen to triumph in the end between Darcy and Elizabeth and the contrast between the first proposal and the second proposal is huge. Both characters are more humble. It is ironic that their love for each other is a secret from everybody else at first, and on admitting to her sister that she loves Darcy, for example, Jane 'looked all amazement' (p. 353) and could only believe she was joking. True love also triumphs between Bingley and Jane in the closing chapters of the novel providing readers, as well as the Bennet family, with a satisfying ending. Volume Three, Chapter XIX (Chapter 61) presents a romantic and reassuring picture of how married life begins for the sisters.

A01

Could have provided a quotation and some analysis

A04

Some understanding of relevant contextual factors but fairly general

Their marriages also bring the sisters property and financial security as well as true love. They have married well as their father and mother in particular had been anxious that they should do. At the time when Jane Austen was writing, money, gender and marriage were very closely linked and Mr Bennet is right to worry about money with his house entailed to a male cousin on his death (because he has no son) and five dowries to pay for (because he has five daughters). Some readers have criticised Mrs Bennet for her obsession with marrying off her daughters, but it could be argued that she is more realistic and practical than her husband who has buried his head in the sand.

A03

Supporting critical quotation would have helped makes this point more strongly

A01

Argument has been developed in a straightforward way

True love triumphs in "Pride and Prejudice". Austen shows the main characters coming through all kinds of complications and confusions and marrying 'well' in every sense of the word.

GRADE C

Comment

A01 Expression, though sometimes lacking fluency, is clear. Addresses the topic but there is a lack of consistent focus on the novel as a literary text.

A03 There is some helpful awareness of how different readers have reacted to the text and some textual support for this. An attempt to give more than one reaction to the statement in the title would have enhanced this essay.

A04 The answer alludes to the novel's social context and makes some relevant if quite general points.

For a B grade

To gain a higher grade, the answer would need to include at least some of the following:
● More evidence of an argument that unfolds and develops as the answer progresses
● Showing that there is more than one way of looking at the statement in the question
● Developed account of the novel's effects with attention to language and structure
● More explicit awareness of the author at work in the text

CANDIDATE 2

A01 Articulate and relevant response

A01 Appropriate use of literary term

A01 Interesting and coherent line of argument

True love can indeed be seen ultimately to triumph in "Pride and Prejudice" and some reviewers have argued that the conclusion to this novel is perhaps the most rewarding and romantic in all Austen's works. However, there are many obstacles along the way to the triumph of true love and it is in these obstacles that much of the novel's more biting social satire lies. Furthermore, we are shown that the notion of true love in itself can be a something of a mirage, as the marriages of Mr and Mrs Bennet and Lydia and Wickham suggest.

A04 Good point, worth developing further

For protagonist Elizabeth, the conclusion of her narrative appears to be a happy – not to mention prosperous – union between two compatible partners: 'the stuff of wish-fulfilment' according to critic Vivien Jones. Jones has also referred to this type of ending as a 'powerful cultural myth', emphasising its seductiveness but also its fictiveness in that it bears little relation to reality. Another feature of the genre is the series of misunderstandings that stand in the way of true love before the novel reaches its happy denouement: Darcy's haughty attitude towards 'strangers' at the Netherfield ball, Elizabeth's misunderstanding of Darcy's role in Bingley and Jane's separation, the severe disapproval of Catherine de Bourgh. It could be argued, however, that it is precisely because these obstacles are overcome that the novel's conclusion does not only celebrate true love, but also celebrates its triumph in the face of considerable challenges. Perhaps one of the best examples of this is in the series of retorts Elizabeth gives to Lady Catherine's demands at Longbourn in Volume Three, Chapter XIV (Chapter 56). It is Elizabeth's strength of character that vanquishes the formidable Lady Catherine, foreshadowed perhaps at Rosings in Volume Two, Chapter VI (Chapter 29) when Elizabeth surprises Lady Catherine with her assured responses.

A03 Interesting use of supportive critical material

A01 Articulate response using correct literary terminology

In the stories of both Lydia and Mrs Bennet we find evidence that what appears to be 'love' may not be 'true'. Both characters mistake beauty and sexual attractiveness for love with unfortunate consequences. We may also recall for how much of the novel our heroine Elizabeth is charmed by Wickham, in other words how close she comes to making a similar mistake. At the beginning of Volume Two, Chapter XIX (Chapter 42), Austen gives us an insight into the Bennets' courtship and into Mr Bennet's subsequent reflections on the state of his marriage, an authorial intervention that makes explicit the view that 'youth and beauty' (p. 228) are not a sufficient basis for marriage. It is also made clear in Volume Three, Chapter VIII (Chapter 50) that a tension steadily grew in the Bennets' marriage over their failure to give birth to a boy who, according to the principle of primogeniture, would have inherited the estate at

A01 Appropriate use of literary term

A04 Good use of contextual detail, could be further developed

Longbourn. This predicament gave rise to the stressful issue of the entailment which, as we can see from Mrs Bennet's reactions to Mr Collins's visit with Charlotte in Volume One, Chapter XXIII (Chapter 23), continues to vex her deeply.

Charlotte Lucas's matrimonial affairs provide an interesting contrast to the others. She enters into marriage with her eyes open to Mr Collins's flaws but she is also acutely aware of the probable alternative of lifelong spinsterhood. Elizabeth is less horrified by her friend's decision when she visits her at Hunsford, seeing that marriage has given her friend new projects and challenges which seem to satisfy her. Austen portrays Charlotte as prioritising security over 'true love' and while the narrator does not criticise this pragmatic and 'prudential' (p. 175) approach, the reader is not led to suppose that Mr Collins will become a changed character through his marriage to Charlotte – 'her cousin's manners were not altered by his marriage' (p. 153). Indeed, throughout the novel, Austen shows us that while a person's impressions of something or someone can be changed, a person's character seems to be more fixed. For example, while Lydia merrily tells her sister in a letter of the mutual 'love' and 'joy' (p. 365) she and Wickham have found, the reader knows about the rather less romantic financial settlement that saved her from complete disgrace at his hands.

I would argue that Austen's novel celebrates true love but it also makes us question what true love really is and what a happy marriage requires as its basis. Austen achieves this through the intricate and sometimes dramatic unfolding of the plot over its three volumes as obstacles are overcome, through characterisation which does not gloss over people's faults and weaknesses, and through some telling authorial interventions on the subjects of love and marriage.

A04 Could have been developed into a fuller contextual point about women's lives

A01 Excellent awareness of the novel as a whole

A01 A convincing and personal conclusion

GRADE A

Comment

A01 There is a clear sense from the opening that the candidate has a grasp of the whole novel and of the question. The answer is shaped by an interesting argument and is expressed in an assured way. Each paragraph deals with a different but relevant topic and incidents, and observations are linked well.

A03 The answer analyses a critic's interpretation of the novel, showing good understanding of the ideas expressed. Points are supported very well by references to the text.

A04 The question is illuminated by a number of references to the historical and social context of the novel.

For an A* grade

To gain a higher grade, the answer might include at least some of the following:

● The argument is well sustained throughout but the conclusion might have been more inventive, adding fresh insight as well as supplying a summary of what has been said. (AO1)

● An approach that compared and evaluated different critical positions in relation to the question would have gained a higher grade. (AO3)

● Further analysis and evaluation of the contexts in which the novel was written could also have enhanced the grade. (AO4)

WORKING THROUGH A TASK

Now it's your turn to work through a task on *Pride and Prejudice*. The key is to:

- Read/decode the task/question
- Plan your points – then expand and link your points
- Draft your answer

TASK TITLE

> 'She was able ... to avoid the kind of exaggeration that threatens to undermine the whole project of fiction.' (Carol Shields) How successfully do you feel Austen avoids exaggeration in *Pride and Prejudice*?

DECODE THE QUESTION: KEY WORDS

exaggeration   = i.e. hyperbole, melodrama, sensationalism

How successfully ...?   = evaluate the writer's success? what are **my** views?

Austen   = a reminder that this is a literary creation

PLAN AND EXPAND

- Key aspect: evidence of 'avoidance of exaggeration'

POINT	EXPANDED POINT	EVIDENCE
Point a *Elizabeth is the novel's centre of consciousness*	*Elizabeth is the novel's 'centre of consciousness', to use Henry James's term. She is generally level-headed and not prone to exaggerated reactions or flights of fancy. The narrator's perspective is closest to Elizabeth's of all the characters, preferring irony and wit to sensation and hyperbole.*	'Elizabeth listened in silence, but was not convinced.' (p. 17) 'Elizabeth was chiefly struck with his extraordinary deference for Lady Catherine, and his kind intention of christening, marrying, and burying his parishioners whenever it was required.' (p. 62)
Point b *Austen mocks the idea of heightened sensibility in the passage about the Lake District*	Different aspects of this point expanded *You fill in*	Quotations 1–2 *You fill in*
Point c *Many of the novel's other main characters are portrayed in psychologically realistic ways*	Different aspects of this point expanded *You fill in*	Quotations 1–2 *You fill in*

- Key aspect: evidence of 'exaggeration'

You come up with three points, and then expand them

POINT	EXPANDED POINT	EVIDENCE
Point a	Expanded: *You fill in*	Quotations 1–2 *You fill in*
Point b	Different aspects of this point expanded *You fill in*	Quotations 1–2 *You fill in*
Point c	Different aspects of this point expanded *You fill in*	Quotations 1–2 *You fill in*

● Conclusion:

POINT	EXPANDED POINT	EVIDENCE
Key final point or overall view *You fill in*	Draw together and perhaps add a final further point to support your view *You fill in*	Final quotation to support your view *You fill in*

DEVELOP FURTHER, THEN DRAFT

Now look back over your draft points and:

● Add further links or connections between the points to develop them further or synthesise what has been said, for example:

> *Elizabeth's outburst to her aunt Mrs Gardiner at the end of Volume Two, Chapter IV (Chapter 27) may seem uncharacteristic in its use of hyperbole and exclamations. Elizabeth is expressing her 'delight!' and 'felicity!' about the proposed tour to the Lakes, a destination closely linked with the Romantic poets Wordsworth and Coleridge. It would appear that Austen is satirising Romantic taste and language in this passage, and that Elizabeth is knowingly exaggerating her reactions and language in order to mock travellers and writers who are more routinely given to such 'effusions'.*

● Decide an order for your points/paragraphs – some may now be linked/connected and therefore **not** in the order of the table above.

Now draft your essay. If you're really stuck you can use the opening paragraph below to get you started.

> *Jane Austen is widely credited with developing the novel into a more coherent and modern literary form. The quotation by Shields states that one of the ways in which Austen achieves this is by avoiding exaggeration, thus suggesting that many early novelists were less successful in avoiding such excesses as sensationalism and hyperbole.*

Once you've written your essay, turn to page 128 for a mark scheme on this question to see how well you've done.

FURTHER QUESTIONS

1) How important are letters in this novel?

2) Compare and contrast the characters of Darcy and Wickham with reference to at least one of the following themes: appearance and reality, the study of character, love and marriage.

3) To what extent would you agree with the statement that Austen satirises the manners, behaviour and beliefs of the people she writes about in *Pride and Prejudice*?

4) Discuss how Austen presents *one* of the following in this novel: soldiers, clergymen, servants.

5) How effective is Austen's use of irony in *Pride and Prejudice*?

6) Is it possible for readers to feel any sympathy for Mrs Bennet in the novel?

7) 'Austen's concerns are too narrow for *Pride and Prejudice* to be considered a great work of literature.' How do you respond to this view?

8) What is significant about Lady Catherine de Bourgh's character and role in *Pride and Prejudice*?

9) Compare and contrast the different views of marriage expressed in the novel.

10) *Pride and Prejudice* features many brothers and sisters. Write about the significance of *three* sibling relationships within the novel as a whole.

11) Consider the importance of secrecy in this novel.

12) To what extent can *Pride and Prejudice* be considered a comedy?

FURTHER READING

Janine Barchas (2012) *Matters of fact in Jane Austen: History, Location and Celebrity*. Johns Hopkins University Press, Baltimore, MA.

Wayne C. Booth (1961) *The Rhetoric of Fiction*. University of Chicago Press, Chicago.

Marilyn Butler (1975/1990) *Jane Austen and the War of Ideas*. Clarendon Press, Oxford.

Marilyn Butler (1981) *Romantics, Rebels and Reactionaries: English Literature and its Background 1760–1830*. Oxford University Press, Oxford.

Paula Byrne (2013) *The Real Jane Austen: A Life in Small Things*. Harper Press, London.

Robert Clark (ed.) (1984) *New Casebooks: 'Sense and Sensibility' and 'Pride and Prejudice'*. Macmillan, Basingstoke.

A useful collection of essays and extracts including Isobel Armstrong's 'Politics, Pride, Prejudice and the Picturesque'.

Helen Fielding (1997) *Bridget Jones' Diary*. Picador, London.

E. M. Forster (1927) *Aspects of the Novel*. Edward Arnold, London.

Sandra M. Gilbert and Susan Gubar (1979) *The Madwoman in the Attic: The Woman Writer and the Nineteenth-Century Literary Imagination*. Yale University Press, New Haven.

Robin Gilmour (1981) *The Idea of the Gentleman in the Victorian Novel*. Allen and Unwin, London.

J. David Grey (ed.) (1986) *The Jane Austen Handbook*. Athlone Press, London.

Contains a wide variety of diverse and interesting material; including 'Characterization in Jane Austen' by John Bayley and a chapter by Norman Page on language.

Barbara Hardy (1975) *A Reading of Jane Austen*. Owen, London.

Arnold Kettle (1951–2) *Introduction to the English Novel*. Hutchinson, London.

Margaret Kirkham (1983) *Jane Austen: Feminism and Fiction*. Harvest, Brighton.

Mary Lascelles (1939) *Jane Austen and her Art*. Oxford University Press, Oxford.

F. R. Leavis (1947) *The Great Tradition*. Chatto and Windus, London.

Deirdre Le Faye (ed.) (1995) *Jane Austen's Letters*. Oxford University Press, Oxford.

Jane Austen's letters are well worth reading.

David Lodge (1966) *Language of Fiction*. Routledge and Kegan Paul, London.

David Lodge (1992) *The Art of Fiction*. Secher and Warburg, London.

D. A. Millar (2003) *Jane Austen, or the Secret of Style*. Princeton University Press, Princeton, NJ.

David Nokes (1997) *Jane Austen*. Fourth Estate, London.

Norman Page (1972) *The Language of Jane Austen*. Clarendon Press, Oxford.

Sue Parrill (2002) *Jane Austen on Film and Television*. McFarland and Company, London.

Mary Poovey (1984) *The Proper Lady and the Woman Writer*. University of Chicago Press, Chicago.

Julia Prewitt Brown (1979) *Jane Austen's Novels*. Harvard University Press, Cambridge, MA.

Salman Rushdie (1983) *Shame*. Cape, London.

Carol Shields (2001) *Jane Austen*. Phoenix, London

B. C. Southam (1968) *Jane Austen: The Critical Heritage*. Routledge, London and New York.

Kathleen Tillotson (1954) *Novels of the Eighteen-Forties*. Clarendon Press, Oxford.

Claire Tomalin (1997) *Jane Austen: A Life*. Viking, London.

Lionel Trilling (1955) *The Opposing Self*. Secher and Warburg, London.

Ian Watt (1957) *The Rise of the Novel*. Hogarth, London.

Fay Weldon (1984) *Letters to Alice On First Reading Jane Austen*. Coronet, London.

John Wiltshire (1992) *Jane Austen and the Body*. Cambridge University Press, Cambridge.

John Wiltshire (2001) *Recreating Jane Austen*. Cambridge University Press, Cambridge.

LITERARY TERMS

abstract nouns see **concrete nouns**

antagonist the opponent of the **protagonist**, the chief character in a play or novel, where two figures are engaged in a struggle with each other

antithesis a rhetorical term referring to the neat pairing of contrasting or opposite ideas in the same sentence

aphorism a generally accepted truth or principle expressed in a short and pithy sentence. Eighteenth-century poetry and prose is rich in aphoristic statements

authorial intervention a moment in a narrative when the narrator 'talks' directly to the reader rather than invisibly representing characters through their actions

bathos a laughable descent from the height of the elevated treatment of a serious subject, to the depths of ordinariness and dullness

canon originally a law of the Church; hence the list of books in the Bible accepted and genuine; and by further extension, those literary works which traditionally compose the 'great works' of a nation's literature. The assumption that some authors are intrinsically 'great' is now disputed, though canonical writers like Shakespeare and Jane Austen tend to feature in school curricula

caricature a grotesque or ludicrous rendering of a character, in art or writing, achieved by the exaggeration of personality traits

centre of consciousness a term given by Henry James to the technique of telling a story wholly or chiefly from the point of view of one individual, though the narrative is still third-person, rather than first-person or autobiographical

characterisation the way in which a writer creates characters so as to attract or repel our sympathy

chronological order events in a literary work are arranged and described in the order in which they occurred, or are imagined to have occurred by the author

circumlocution words and descriptions which take roundabout ways of approaching or hinting at a subject rather than addressing it directly, either for comic or ironic effect, or to avoid embarrassing topics

concrete nouns are words representing things and solid objects, such as 'hat', 'horse', or 'hazelnut', as opposed to **abstract nouns** which stand for intangible ideas or feelings like 'happiness', 'history', 'hate', 'hope', etc.

dialogue the speech and conversation of characters in any literary work

direct speech words or sentences that report thought or speech exactly as it was expressed by a character. It is usually enclosed in quotation marks

dramatic irony a common effect in drama (and by extension in novels too), referring to those moments when the audience (or reader) knows more about the circumstances and perhaps future of the characters that are being represented than those characters themselves do

epistolary novel a novel in which the story is told entirely through letters sent by those participating in or observing the events

extended metaphor an extended or elaborate concept that forges an unexpected connection between two apparently dissimilar things. Also known as a 'conceit'

figurative language decorative language that departs from the plainest expression of meaning, by using 'figures of speech'. These are grammatical forms or ways of achieving expression or description that create those patterns or special effects which are common in literary writing. As **metaphor** is one of the commonest figures of speech, 'figurative language' sometimes refers to metaphorical language

foreground a term related to art, where some part of a picture is placed at the front of the imagined space perceived by the viewer. In literature a similar effect may be created by some special and noticeable feature of the language, such as a **metaphor** or similar figure of speech, or by its position in the literary work

foreshadow the capacity of a narrative to hint at or presage future events

free indirect thought or **speech** or **style** or **discourse** a way of representing a character's speech or thought that is neither **direct speech** with inverted commas, nor reported speech with the paraphernalia of 'he said that …' etc.

Thought expressed as direct speech: 'I must be collected and calm,' she thought.

Thought expressed as reported speech: She thought that she ought to be collected and calm.

Thought expressed in free indirect style: She must be collected and calm.

Gothic a genre of writing which has a number of typical elements such as ghosts, horror, sublime landscapes

implied reader every text contains features which hint at or imply the kind of reader at which it is aimed. These features may be to do with subject matter, tone of voice, assumptions as to shared interests and knowledge, etc.

intertextuality the explicit or implicit referencing of other texts within a work of literature. It is designed to put the work in the context of other literary works and traditions and implies parallels between them

irony saying one thing while you mean another. A capacity for irony indicates a disposition to see things from several points of view (see also pp. 97–8)

juxtaposition the technique of placing two or more seemingly unrelated ideas next to each other in a text, creating meaning from the interaction of the differences and similarities between them

melodrama sensational drama, emotionally exaggerated

metaphor a figure of speech in which an idea, action or thing is said actually to be something else, drawing out a resemblance between the two. Common in everyday speech – calling someone a 'rat' or a 'drone' or a 'flower' is metaphorical – and in literary writing, especially poetry

motif a topic raised at several points in a literary work, of lesser significance than a **theme**. Dancing, walking, reading, letter-writing, clothes and food all serve as motifs in *Pride and Prejudice*. Characters are distinguished from each other by their attitudes to such interests or activities

narrator the voice telling the story or relating a sequence of events

omniscient narrator the narrator of a story who knows in a godlike way every detail of the characters' lives, their motives, intentions, desires, thoughts, actions, etc.

paradox an apparently self-contradictory statement, or one that seems in conflict with logic or opinion, yet expressing a meaning or truth behind the seeming absurdity

parody an imitation of a specific work of literature, or literary **style** or genre, devised so as to ridicule its characteristic features

plot the plan of a literary work, suggesting the pattern of relationships between events

protagonist the chief character in a play or novel, now almost synonymous with 'hero' or 'heroine', who may be locked in a struggle with the villain, or **antagonist**. A word from Greek drama

pun a play on words, often for comic effect, on different senses of the same word or on similar-sounding words

realism a difficult and often vague term. Realism has come to refer to novels that attempt to describe characters in relation to their society, and therefore proceed with the premise that this attempt is possible and worthwhile. The characters and society are assumed to be 'normal' and examples of 'ordinary life', though such concepts are matters of dispute

register the kind of language being used; i.e. the degree of formality, the vocabulary and syntax

rhetorical question a question asked not for the sake of enquiry but for emphasis: the writer or speaker expects the reader or audience to be totally convinced about the appropriate reply

satire literature which exhibits or examines vice and folly and makes them appear ridiculous or contemptible

social comedy comedy with an upper-class setting, noted for witty dialogue rather than physical jokes

style the characteristic manner in which a writer expresses herself or himself, or the particular manner of an individual literary work or specific literary character

subtext the situation that lies behind the behaviour of the characters in a play or novel, but which is not referred to or explained explicitly

theme the abstract subject of a literary work: its central idea or ideas

TIMELINE

WORLD EVENTS	AUTHOR'S LIFE	LITERARY EVENTS
		1740 Samuel Richardson, *Pamela*, or *Virtue Rewarded* **1748** Samuel Richardson, *Clarissa*, **1749** Henry Fielding, *The History of Tom Jones, a Foundling*
1760 George III accedes to the throne	**1760** George Austen, Jane Austen's father, takes up trusteeship of a plantation in Antigua	
1773 The 'Boston Tea Party': workers in Boston protest against British attempts to tax the American Colonies	**1775** Birth of Jane Austen at Steventon, Hampshire	**1778** Fanny Burney, *Evelina*
1783 American independence is finally recognised by Britain		**1788** First edition of *The Times* newspaper
1789 Outbreak of the French Revolution; George Washington becomes first president of the United States of America	**1790** *Love and Friendship* finished	
1792 France is declared a republic **1793** France declares war on Britain during the ongoing French Revolutionary Wars; executions of Louis XVI and Marie Antoinette		**1794** Ann Radcliffe, *The Mysteries of Udolpho*; William Blake, *Songs of Innocence and Experience*; Prince Hoare, *My Grandmother* **1796** Matthew 'Monk' Lewis, *The Monk*
	1797 *First Impressions* is rejected for publication; later rewritten as *Pride and Prejudice* **1797–8** An earlier work, *Elinor and Marianne*, is rewritten as *Sense and Sensibility*	**1797** Anne Radcliffe, *The Italian*
1800–15 The Napoleonic Wars in Europe: a continuation of the French Revolutionary Wars led by Napoleon Bonaparte **1801** The Act of Union creating the United Kingdom of Great Britain and Ireland comes into force	**1801** George Austen retires to Bath with his wife and two daughters **1802** Jane Austen turns down Harris Bigg-Wither's proposal of marriage **1805** Death of George Austen; Jane Austen abandons *The Watsons*	**1802** The Pic Nic Society of dilettanti aristocratic amateur actors formed by Albinia, Countess of Buckinghamshire
1805 Nelson defeats a combined French and Spanish fleet at the battle of Trafalgar **1807–8** Abolition Act outlaws Britain's slave trade **1808–14** Peninsular War in Spain between France and Britain	**1809** Jane Austen settles at Chawton with her mother and sister Cassandra **1811** *Sense and Sensibility* published; Jane Austen starts work on *Mansfield Park*	**1807** George Crabbe, *The Parish Register* **1808** Johann Wolfgang von Goethe, *Faust, Part I* **1809** First edition of the *Quarterly Review* published
1811 King George III suffers his final attack of illness **1812** The Prince of Wales becomes Prince Regent **1814** Allies invade France; Napoleon abdicates and retires to Elba **1815** Napoleon escapes from Elba to march on Paris, becoming Emperor again, only to be defeated by Wellington at the battle of Waterloo **1815–23** John Nash builds Brighton Pavilion at the request of the Prince Regent	**1813** *Pride and Prejudice* published **1814** First publication of *Mansfield Park*; Jane Austen begins *Emma* **1815** Sir Walter Scott reviews *Emma* for the Quarterly Review **1816** *Emma* published; second edition of *Mansfield Park* appears; Henry, Jane Austen's brother, is declared bankrupt; Jane begins *Persuasion* in failing health **1817** Death of Jane Austen at Winchester; *Sanditon* left unfinished; *Persuasion* and *Northanger Abbey* published posthumously	**1812** George Crabbe, *Tales in Verse* **1817** Walter Scott, *Rob Roy*; Lord Byron, *Manfred*
		1818 Mary Shelley, *Frankenstein* **1819** Walter Scott, *Ivanhoe*; Lord Byron, *Don Juan*
1820 Death of George III; the Prince Regent accedes as George IV		

REVISION FOCUS TASK ANSWERS

TASK 1

Austen, like Darcy, has 'a very satirical eye'.

- While the story Austen tells in *Pride and Prejudice* is essentially a romantic one, much of the novel's interest and entertainment are more in the vein of social comedy.

- Austen's narration is peppered with revealing details and witty asides.

- Examples of Austen's 'satirical eye' include her presentation of the novel's only cleric Mr Collins and the knowing way in which matters about social class and status are handled.

Charlotte's views on love, courtship and marriage are of vital importance for the novel as a whole.

- Charlotte is seen from early in the novel to have very pragmatic and perhaps cynical views about love and marriage.

- Her views about how far a young woman should make it clear to her suitor that she returns his affections are strongly disputed by Elizabeth. But Charlotte's concerns are later seen to have foreshadowed the problems encountered by Bingley and Jane.

- Charlotte's marriage to Mr Collins brings her security but not love. By her own standards if not by Elizabeth's she has made a successful match.

TASK 2

Austen depicts family life in both positive and negative ways.

- There are several close relationships between family members (such as Elizabeth and Jane, Darcy and Georgiana, and the Gardiners) depicted in the novel.

- The novel also shows us some less attractive aspects of family life such as interference, favouritism and quarrelling.

- By examining courtship as well as more established married couples and their offspring over the course of the novel, Austen is able to suggest to the reader what does and what doesn't make a sound foundation for marriage and family life.

The relationship between marriage and money is thoroughly explored in *Pride and Prejudice*.

- From the very beginning, marriage and money are inextricably linked in this novel, as shown by Mrs Bennet's determination to pay a visit to the newly arrived Bingley who is rumoured to be in possession of a 'large fortune'.

- Lydia's marriage settlement saves her from further disgrace. This is a particularly stark and perhaps, to modern readers, unsettling example of the financial settlements that accompanied a marriage at this time.

- We are also shown in the novel how marriage can be a woman's route to a degree of independence and security and, indeed, to upward social mobility.

TASK 3

Pemberley is presented to the reader very differently to the other homes in the novel.

- The account of the visit to Darcy's home is detailed and reads like a tour in itself.

- The reader sees the house through Elizabeth's eyes and understands the powerful impression the house and its owner make on her.

- A strong connection is made between Darcy and Pemberley; the house could be seen to symbolise many of his own qualities: handsome, wealthy but revealing a hatred of artifice and showiness.

The reader has intimate access to Elizabeth's thoughts and feelings throughout the novel and consequently is more sympathetic towards her than towards Darcy.

- When Darcy and Elizabeth first meet, we see events principally through Elizabeth's eyes, and may sympathise with those characters who find him proud and haughty.

- Austen gives us occasional access to Darcy's feelings: sometimes indirectly (for example, when he is described as looking intently at Elizabeth) and sometimes directly (for example, his long letter to Elizabeth).

- However, Elizabeth is the novel's centre of consciousness and the reader accompanies her through her experiences and impressions of events and characters. She is not always right but her openness and self-knowledge are attractive qualities in a protagonist.

TASK 4

Financial prudence is an important virtue in _Pride and Prejudice_.

- Wickham's spendthrift ways are indicative of his reckless behaviour.

- Mr Bennet berates himself for not having been more financially prudent.

- While the first thing we learn about Darcy is his wealth, it is more gradually revealed to Elizabeth and to the reader that Darcy is also a financially prudent and considerate master, landlord and friend.

The words 'pride' and 'prejudice' can be applied to a number of characters in the novel.

- Lady Catherine may be seen as an embodiment of both pride and prejudice, judging people more on their social class than on their character.

- Lydia's giddy mood and flirtatious behaviour may be seen as pride before a fall.

- Caroline Bingley and her sister could be viewed as prejudiced against the Bennet family, despite their initial friendliness towards Jane. Austen describes the sisters as 'proud and conceited' and suggests they may feel insecure in their social position since their father made his fortune in trade.

TASK 5

Austen's omniscient narration is judgemental but even-handed; she exposes weaknesses and flaws in each of her characters.

- Austen's omniscient narrative style means that she reveals details about characters not only through dialogue and physical description but also through directly describing for readers a character's qualities and foibles.

- Austen may at times be seen to ridicule some characters (Mrs Bennet, Mr Collins, Lady Catherine), usually for comic effect.

- Being a good judge of character is a central and highly valued idea in this novel. Austen shows us the irony of this when characters fail to see for themselves what the narrator shows us more clearly.

Despite the obstacles they have to overcome, Austen shows Elizabeth and Darcy to be well-matched from the beginning of the novel.

- From the start, Darcy and Elizabeth seem a good match for each other's intelligence and wit.

- Even when Darcy and Elizabeth antagonise each other, their verbal sparring is exciting to read.

- At the end of the novel, Darcy and Elizabeth talk at length and deepen their understanding of each other's character and behaviour.

MARK SCHEME

Use this page to assess your answer to the Worked task, provided on pages 120–1.

Aiming for an A grade? Fulfil all the criteria below and your answer should hit the mark.*

> 'She was able ... to avoid the kind of exaggeration that threatens to undermine the whole project of fiction' (Carol Shields). How successfully do you feel Austen avoids exaggeration in *Pride and Prejudice*?

AO1	Articulate creative, informed and relevant responses to literary texts, using appropriate terminology and concepts, and coherent, accurate written expression.	• You make a range of clear, relevant points about Austen's avoidance of exaggeration in *Pride and Prejudice*. • You write a balanced essay exploring how far you agree with Shields's statement. • You use a range of literary terms correctly, e.g. **melodrama**, **irony**, **parody**, **narrator**. • You write a clear introduction, outlining your thesis, and provide a clear conclusion. • You signpost and link your ideas about exaggeration, *Pride and Prejudice* and the novel.
AO2	Demonstrate detailed critical understanding in analysing the ways in which structure, form and language shape meanings in literary texts.	• You explain the techniques and methods Austen uses to construct *Pride and Prejudice*, and link them to main themes of the text. • You may discuss, for example, how Elizabeth is presented as the novel's 'centre of consciousness' and we are led to view others through her eyes. • You explain in detail how your examples affect meaning, e.g. Austen's presentation of Elizabeth as an astute and reasonable observer of human behaviour ('Elizabeth could not but smile at such a conclusion of such a beginning; but Mrs Bennet ... was excessively disappointed' (Vol. One, Ch. XX (Ch. 20), p. 110) creates a contrast for the reader with her presentation of the more extreme and unreflective minor characters such as Elizabeth's own mother and youngest sisters. • You may explore how other aspects, such as the setting – not only descriptions of family homes but also references to shops, inns and military quarters – are used by Austen to construct a realistic world.
AO3	Explore connections and comparisons between different literary texts, informed by interpretations of other readers.	• You make relevant links between Austen's style and that of other authors of the time. • When appropriate, you compare the use/avoidance of exaggeration in *Pride and Prejudice* with the role of exaggeration in other novels, e.g. the **Gothic** novels that were popular before and during the time when Austen was writing. • You incorporate and comment on other critics' views of *Pride and Prejudice* and the techniques Austen uses. • You assert your own independent view clearly.
AO4	Demonstrate understanding of the significance and influence of the contexts in which literary texts are written and received.	You explain how relevant aspects of the social, literary and historical contexts of *Pride and Prejudice* are significant when examining Austen's style. For example, you may discuss: • Literary context: Through the character of Elizabeth, Austen can be seen to satirise popular Romantic depictions of nature and heightened emotion. • Historical context: Mrs Bennet's obsession with seeing her daughters married is in part a reflection of the huge financial and social importance to a family of daughters marrying well. • Social context: Austen's treatment of Mr Collins does not reveal the clergy in a positive light. He is presented as a caricature, seen to be more interested in his own social standing than the welfare of his parishioners, and his attitude towards Lydia is particularly harsh and unforgiving.

* This mark scheme gives you a broad indication of attainment, but check the specific mark scheme for your paper/task to ensure you know what to focus on.